The Mediterranean Diet Cookbook
for Healthy Living

The Mediterranean Diet Cookbook for Healthy Living

115 Fresh and Easy Recipes with
28 Days of Meal Plans

Marilyn Haugen

ISBN-13 978-0-9982470-1-4
Madison, WI
Aperio Publishing
FoodThymes.com

Manufactured in the United States of America

Table of Contents

FOREWARD

In a world fixated on fad diets, super-foods, and magical supplements, the need for sound nutrition advice has never been greater. The truth is that there is no instant path to weight loss or a magic pill to give you that perfect figure. On the other hand, neither do you need to spend your entire salary on organically sourced roots from a place on the map you cannot even pronounce to be healthy! The reality is the human body requires balance; diets that eliminate or overemphasize certain food groups may appear to be beneficial but can cause damage in the long run. Marilyn Haugen brings readers back to the basics by using an eating style called the Mediterranean diet. Rather than a strict list of dos and do nots, this ideology focuses on sound nutritional principles, a well-rounded diet and flexibility to meet the needs of individual people. Barring any special dietary circumstances, we in the field of nutrition readily recommend this diet to anyone looking to eat healthier.

One of the greatest barriers we have observed in people trying to change their diets is the mindset of feeling restricted, deprived, and even punished by their food plans. Haugen does a wonderful job of fighting this mentality by showing readers that eating better is an opportunity to try new and amazing foods. Her recipes are flavorful and in the spirit of recognizing that not all people are alike, encourages readers to innovate if ingredients are hard to find or not to the readers' liking. If past attempts at eating healthier have failed for any of these reasons, this book might be exactly what you are looking for. Haugen's approach is exciting, just like eating should be!

- Alexander Kim, MS
  New York City, New York
  B.A. Cornell University
  M.S. The Institute of Human Nutrition at Columbia University

THE MEDITERRANEAN DIET PRIMER

Are you ready to take a trip to the Mediterranean from the comfort of your kitchen? You will be indulging in an abundance of fruits, vegetables, whole grains, legumes and healthy oils from fish and nuts. Your meals will be easy to prepare, mouth-watering and good for you. Sounds wonderful doesn't it! The Mediterranean Diet and the recipes and meal plans in this cookbook will most certainly take you there.

The Mediterranean Diet is much more than just a *diet*, it is an approach to healthier eating, enjoying mealtimes and physical activity. The diet is built around the eating patterns of the countries surrounding the Mediterranean Sea. For decades, researchers have recognized that the people of these regions experienced a longer lifespan and a decrease in cardiovascular disease. Your Doctor may already have recommended the Mediterranean Diet to you to decrease your risks of heart disease, dementia and other chronic diseases. One of the most intriguing aspects of this diet is that is does not require a strict set of foods that must be consumed or avoided, as in many trendy diets. This lifestyle approach to healthy eating emphasizes consuming proportionately more fruits, vegetables, legumes, whole grains, lean protein and healthy fats than sweets and red meats. While sweets and red meat are consumed in small amounts and less frequently, they are not foods you need to avoid entirely. At the core of the Mediterranean way of eating, is that no foods are eliminated but the proportion and frequency of food groups changes to provide you with a healthy diet.

While the thought of consuming increased amounts of vegetables and fruits may seem daunting, with proper preparation and variety, the meals become much more flavorful and satisfying. There is something for everyone in this diet, including foods for picky eaters and kids. Engaging everyone in the household in trying new recipes, preparing meals, enjoying those meals together and eating at a leisurely pace is a great way to transition to a healthier lifestyle with the Mediterranean Diet.

Healthy Eating Patterns

Before I dive into the specifics behind the diet, think about this path you are embarking on as changing some of the foods you eat and in what proportions you eat them. Dieting implies to many of us what we will be giving up all the foods we love. The Mediterranean way of eating is not an all or nothing plan. Knowing that it's okay if some days things just don't work out as planned will help you not feel discouraged or ready to abandon this healthy eating style.

Don't think about this as a 'diet' per se, but a chance to indulge in fresh, sweet fruits, colorful seasonal vegetables bursting with flavors, delectable seafood, fish, poultry and lean meats, hearty grains and beans bursting with texture and taste, and fresh herbs and spices that bring out the best of anything on your table. Picture the rich and abundant coastline of Mediterranean countries. Then imagine the bounty of foods enjoyed for thousands of years by the people of Greece, Italy, Spain, North Africa and France. With those things in mind, you should begin to appreciate the culinary adventure you are about to take.

Not only has this way of eating been enjoyed for the ages by this region of the world, but it also aligns perfectly with the USDA's *Dietary Guidelines for Americans*. With this healthy eating pattern, you will be enjoying:

- Daily meals that include vegetables, fruits- especially whole fruits, whole grains, legumes, nuts and seeds.

- Low-fat or no-fat dairy products such as yogurt, milk and aged cheese.

- Seafood and fish with a wonderful balance of nutrients including Omega-3's.

- Moderate amounts of poultry and eggs.

- Red meats and desserts, but with lesser frequency than you may be used to.

- Herbs and seasonings that not only add flavor and contribute to the uniqueness of Mediterranean cuisine but add to the 'superpower' makeup of these foods.

- Healthy oils, including those from plants, nuts, and seeds, and those occurring naturally in foods such as seafood, olives, and avocados.

Food and mealtimes are meant to be enjoyed which can easily be accomplished with the Mediterranean lifestyle and can also contribute to a healthier you.

Recommended Accessories

Aside from some standard kitchen utensils, there are a few other kitchen gadgets that you will need (or will find handy) when preparing the recipes in this book.

- **Large chef's knife:** A sharp chef's knife is the best tool for cutting fruit, vegetables and meats for almost any recipe.

- **Garlic roller and press:** This are two of my favorite gadgets. A silicone garlic roller makes peeling your garlic incredibly easy. While you can certainly mince garlic by hand, a garlic press makes this frequent task a snap.

- **Standard measuring cups and spoons:** Use a glass measuring cup with a spout to measure liquids. Use nesting-style dry measuring cups to measure dry and moist ingredients. Measuring spoons can be used to measure both dry and liquid ingredient.

- **Digital kitchen scale:** For a high degree of accuracy, a digital kitchen scale gives you precise weights for your ingredients. A measurement conversion chart is included in the back of this book for help in converting ingredients.

- **Instant-read thermometer:** This is the best tool for making sure your meats and poultry are properly cooked.
- **Kitchen gloves:** A pair of kitchen gloves is very useful when you're handling hot peppers, certain spices and fruits or vegetables that can stain your hands.
- **Sieve:** A fine-mesh sieve is useful for straining liquids, and rinsing rice and beans.
- **Electric mixer:** Either a stand mixer or a handheld mixer can be used; either make it much easier to mix ingredients.
- **Blender or food processor:** A stand blender is useful for making smoothies and puréeing ingredients for sauces. In many instances, if you don't have a blender, large food processor will work well

The Mediterranean Pantry

All of the ingredients in the recipes are readily available in grocery stores, so shopping for ingredients will be just as easy as cooking them. In addition, many of the recipes use nonperishable items and/or frozen foods so you can cook a meal without going to the store — provided you keep your pantry and freezer well-stocked, of course!

Following are some staples, used in a large number of the recipes, that you will want to be sure to keep on hand:

Herbs, Seasonings and Flavorings

When adding fresh or dried herbs, seasonings and flavorings, remember that a little goes a long way. Always use the amount specified in the recipe for the best flavor and consistency. If you are confident in your cooking skills and are familiar with a recipe, you may want to adjust the type or amount of these ingredients. Make any changes in small increments.

Some dishes call for seasonings such as Ras el Hanout or Harissa. These are seasoning blends. If you don't want to purchase them specifically or don't have them on hand, they can be created by using other seasonings in your pantry.

Olive Oil

Olive oils are used in many of the recipes in this book since it is a healthier oil. Virgin olive oil is a better (and less expensive) choice for recipes that are cooked, as it has a higher smoke point than extra virgin olive oil. The high quality and superior taste of extra virgin olive oil make it the best choice for salads and other recipes that are not cooked at high temperatures.

Vinegars

Vinegar can impact the texture, color, flavor and thickness of dishes, adding acidity and sourness that can increase our enjoyment of our food. There are many types of vinegar, each of which has its own unique flavor. The vinegars used in this book include balsamic vinegar, apple cider vinegar and red or white wine vinegar. If you are unsure which ones to have on hand, start with whichever one is used in a recipe you want to make, then expand your pantry provisions from there.

Canned and Frozen Vegetables and Fruits

Eating an abundance of vegetables and fruits is key to a healthy diet. They also help make you feel full faster. With seasonal limitations and perishability, fresh may not always be an option. Canned or frozen fruits and vegetables increase your options for adding these to your diet. Chose ones that are free from salt, sugar and additives.

Fish and Seafood

By far one of the primary sources of omega-3s in your diet, fish is recognized by the American Medical Association as reducing the likelihood of death from health-related causes if consumed 2 to 3 times per week. Fresh fish is always good to pick up from your local fish monger as they can help you decide on different varieties that suit both your taste and budget. Frozen and canned fish and seafood is also great to have on hand as it can help in preparing quick and easy meals.

Legumes

Beans at an abundance of nutrients and fiber to your meal. They are relatively inexpensive and can increase the amount of servings per recipe without adding a higher proportion of other ingredients. Both dry and canned beans are fine to use. If using dried beans, cook up a large batch ahead of time – they freeze well and can be stored in measured amounts for a quick and easy meal. Canned beans should be drained and rinsed well before using.

Rice and Grains

These ingredients are found throughout the recipes in this book and are at the core of the Mediterranean Diet. If you haven't tried or heard of a specific variety, give it a try – you may be pleasantly surprised at the result.

Pasta

Pasta is another core ingredient in the regions of the Mediterranean. Use a whole-wheat or protein-enriched pasta for more nutrient-rich meals.

Nuts and Seeds

Both of these ingredients add variety and flavor to your dishes, along with being a power-house of good nutrients. They are also wonderful as a quick and easy pick-me-up snack. Freezing nuts is a good way to keep them fresh longer.

Lemons and Limes

Fresh lemon and lime zest and juice is called for in many recipes, but they may not be always easy to have on hand. Bottled, refrigerated juices are also fine to use. You can freeze leftover zest for future use. I always have on hand dried lemon, lime and orange zest that I can quickly rehydrate for any recipe.

Salt and Pepper

Kosher and sea salt are the first choice of salts to use for flavor and seasoning as they make a bigger contribution to the taste of the recipe without adding a lot of sodium. Regular table salt can be used if you don't have the others on hand, but decrease the amount called for in the recipe by at least two-thirds.

Freshly ground black pepper yields much better flavor and results than pre-ground pepper, but you can use whichever you have on hand.

> It's a good idea to measure out ingredients ahead of time. This is a great way to speed up your cooking and make sure you have everything ready to use when you need it.

Meal Planning and Preparation

To make it much easier for you to get started with your Mediterranean meals, I have included 28 days of complete meal plans to get you started. These are not hard and fast plans or rules, just like the Mediterranean lifestyle isn't a fixed, rule-following diet. The daily plans are there to make it easier for planning, meal preparation and grocery shopping. There are also planned leftovers in many days so you don't have to prepare or cook all of your meals.

The daily and weekly plans are designed to provide you with approximately 1500 to 1600 calories per day, of which the nutritional content is 50 percent carbohydrates, 30 percent fat and 20 percent protein. These recommendations apply to adults 19 years and older with moderate levels of activity. Because the Mediterranean diets can be highly individualized, your actual intake may vary.

I've also created the meal plans so you can increase the amounts of certain recipes or ingredients, or even enjoy a glass of wine! It is not recommended that you eat less than the suggested calories.

The meal plans are there to give you a quick start on your Mediterranean diet. You can always mix or match the individual recipes to suit your tastes.

It's Time to Get Food on the Table!

Once you have decided on a recipe you want to prepare, scan the ingredient and equipment lists to make sure you have everything you need on hand and read the recipe all the way through before you start, to avoid unexpected surprises like necessary marinating or refrigeration time. For best results, purchase fresh vegetables, fruits, herbs, fish, and poultry just before you want to use them or, at the most, 2 to 3 days ahead.

Quick Tips for Success

You will have the most success with your dishes if you have all of the ingredients prepped and ready to go before you start following the recipe steps (unless otherwise directed in the method).

- Measure ingredients carefully for optimal results.
- Follow the recipe steps in the order listed.
- Clean all work surfaces and hands before and after preparing ingredients, especially for fresh fish and poultry.

28 DAYS OF COMPLETE MEAL PLANS

To get you started enjoying all the benefits of the Mediterranean lifestyle, the following pages contain 4 weeks of complete meal plans using core ingredients of the Mediterranean diet. Included are Mediterranean recipes for breakfast, lunch, dinner, desserts and snacks. The meal plans include recipes from this cookbook, including planned leftovers. A handful of staples are included in the plans so you don't feel like you are preparing a meal for every time and day of the week.

These daily plans use nutritional recommendations for the number of calories and macro-nutrients that are the healthiest and do not compromise safety, according to US News Best Diets expert panel. Each meal plan includes calories and nutrients for recipes, individual meals, and a daily total.

Because every person will have individualized needs, your actual intake will vary. Also, there will be days where it is easier than others for you to follow these recommendations. Any and all of this is okay.

One of the key factors is that the diet has recommendations for healthy food groups, not restrictive, unusual foods that 'must' be eaten.

Daily Calorie Needs: According to the US Department of Health and Human Services (DHS) Office of Disease Prevention and Health Promotion, "the estimated daily calorie needs range from 1,600 to 2,400 calories per day for adult women and 2,000 to 3,000 calories per day for adult men. Within each age and sex category, the low end of the range is for sedentary individuals; the high end of the range is for active individuals."

On average, a woman needs to eat about 2000 calories per day to maintain, and 1500 calories to lose one pound of weight per week. An average man needs 2500 calories to maintain, and 2000 to lose one pound of weight per week.

The key to losing weight is to consume fewer calories than your body expends in a day.

The Mediterranean Diet Plan

For the typical Mediterranean Diet, the recommended guidelines are approximately 1527 calories per day with 50 percent coming from carbohydrates, 30 percent from fat, and 20 percent from protein. Additionally, carbohydrates should include about 32 grams of fiber. Fiber is included for those who would like to track their net carbohydrates.

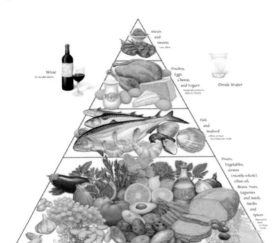

Using these guidelines in conjunction with those supplied above by DHS, the average adult female could lose about 1 lb per week. The **Complete Meal Plans** that follow, give you the ability to add servings, make substitutions, have a glass of wine with dinner or to make other changes that suit your needs.

The meal plans are here to get you started and to give you a realistic picture of what a day, week or month of eating Mediterranean looks like. You will find that some days have more or fewer calories or a varying percentage of nutrients, but the days on average over time will be consistent with the overall goals.

LET'S GET STARTED!

WEEK 1

Day 1 - 1568 Calories • 197g Carbs (48g Fiber) • 64g Fat • 74g Protein

Breakfast	Lunch	Dinner	Snack
379 Cal	472 Cal	442 Cal	275 Cal
Asparagus and Mushroom Frittata	**Quinoa Edamame Toss**	**Hearty Lasagna with Lentils and Zucchini**	**Make-It-Your-Own Fruit, Nut and Seed Bars**
1 serving • 326 Cal	1 serving • 472 Cal	1 serving • 331 Cal	1 serving • 217 Cal
Strawberries	(Make leftovers)	**Cantaloupe**	(Make leftovers)
1 cup sliced • 53 Cal		2 slices • 47 Cal	**Peaches**
		Raspberries	1 medium • 59 Cal
		1 cup • 64 Cal	

Day 2 - 1580 Calories • 191g Carbs (29g Fiber) • 64g Fat • 79g Protein

Breakfast	Lunch	Dinner	Snack
193 Cal	576 Cal	594 Cal	217 Cal
Overnight Oatmeal with Fruit and Yogurt	**Quinoa Edamame Toss**	**Chicken, Peppers and Red Onion Kabobs**	**Make-It-Your-Own Fruit, Nut and Seed Bars**
1 serving • 193 Cal	1 serving • 472 Cal	1 serving • 410 Cal	1 serving • 217 Cal
	(From leftovers)	**Mixed fruit**	(From leftovers)
	Grapes	3/4 cup • 184 Cal	
	1 cup • 104 Cal		

Day 3 - 1537 Calories • 205 Carbs (45g Fiber) • 57g Fat • 73g Protein

Breakfast	Lunch	Dinner	Snack
414 Cal	353 Cal	518 Cal	253 Cal
Quinoa and Feta Egg Muffins	**Easy Creamy Hummus**	**Salmon Provençal with Fennel and Orange**	**Baba Ghanouj**
2 muffins • 225 Cal	1 serving • 266 Cal	1 serving • 328 Cal	1 serving • 240 Cal
(Make leftovers)	**Baby carrots**	**Rice Pilaf**	**Celery**
Banana	1 cup • 86 Cal	1/3 of a box • 190 Cal	2 stalks • 13 Cal
1 medium • 105 Cal			
Blueberries			
1 cup • 84 Cal			

Day 4 - 1552 Calories • 144g Carbs (24g Fiber) • 69g Fat • 100g Protein

Breakfast	Lunch	Dinner	Snack
319 Cal	386 Cal	747 Cal	101 Cal
Quinoa and Feta Egg Muffins	**Tuna, Green Beans and Tomatoes with Shells**	**Sirloin Ribbons**	**Peanut butter**
2 muffins • 225 Cal	1 serving • 386 Cal	1 serving • 342 Cal	1 tbsp • 94 Cal
(From leftovers)	(Make leftovers)	**Lebanese Potatoes**	**Celery**
Apple		1 serving • 237 Cal	1 stalk • 6 Cal
1 apple • 95 Cal		**Braised Green Beans with Mint and Feta**	
		1 serving • 168 Cal	

Day 5 - 1542 Calories • 209g Carbs (22g Fiber) • 45g Fat • 84g Protein

Breakfast	Lunch	Dinner	Snack
347 Cal	386 Cal	594 Cal	216 Cal
Crustless Market Vegetable Quiche	**Tuna, Green Beans and Tomatoes with Shells**	**Farfalle with Creamy Tomato Avocado Sauce**	**Nonfat Greek yogurt**
1 serving • 230 Cal	1 serving • 386 Cal	1 serving • 361 Cal	1 cup • 142 Cal
(Make leftovers)	(From leftovers)	(Make leftovers)	**Mangos**
Blueberries		**Yogurt Panna Cotta with Honey**	3/4 cup sliced • 74 Cal
1 cup • 84 Cal		1 serving • 232 Cal	
Raspberries			
1/2 cup • 32 Cal			

Day 6 - 1569 Calories • 199g Carbs (28g Fiber) • 64g Fat • 61g Protein

Breakfast	Lunch	Dinner	Snack
228 Cal	361 Cal	656 Cal	324 Cal
Plain yogurt	**Farfalle with Creamy**	**Pork Chops with**	**Fruit Cup Chia**
1 cup • 154 Cal	**Tomato Avocado Sauce**	**Vegetable Medley**	**Pudding**
Grapefruit	1 serving • 361 Cal	1 serving • 258 Cal	1 serving • 324 Cal
1 grapefruit • 74 Cal	(From leftovers)	**Cauliflower Couscous**	
		1 serving • 398 Cal	
		(Make leftovers)	

Day 7 - 1545 Calories • 156g Carbs (23g Fiber) • 73g Fat • 77g Protein

Breakfast	Lunch	Dinner	Snack
284 Cal	398 Cal	647 Cal	217 Cal
Crustless Market	**Cauliflower Couscous**	**Seared Salmon with**	**Cottage cheese**
Vegetable Quiche	1 serving • 398 Cal	**Salsa Verde**	3/4 cup • 122 Cal
1 serving • 230 Cal	(From leftovers)	1 serving • 370 Cal	**Apple**
(From leftovers)		**Blood Orange Salad**	1 apple • 95 Cal
Strawberries		**with Lemon-**	
1 cup, sliced • 53 Cal		**Vinaigrette**	
(166 g)		1 serving • 276 Cal	

WEEK 2

Day 8 - 1589 Calories • 183g Carbs (27g Fiber) • 56g Fat • 101g Protein

Breakfast	Lunch	Dinner	Snack
478 Cal	209 Cal	682 Cal	220 Cal
Shakshuka	**Kale with Raisins and**	**Paella Valenciana**	**Pita bread**
1 serving • 414 Cal	**Pine Nuts**	1 serving • 517 Cal	1 large pita • 170 Cal
Raspberries	1 serving • 209 Cal	**Strawberry Topped**	**Tzatziki Sauce**
1 cup • 64 Cal (123 g)		**Almond Cake**	1 serving • 50 Cal
		1 serving • 165 Cal	

Day 9 - 1556 Calories • 201g Carbs (35g Fiber) • 60g Fat • 69g Protein

Breakfast	Lunch	Dinner	Snack
215 Cal	432 Cal	597 Cal	312 Cal
Broccoli Cheddar Egg	**Freekeh with Chickpeas,**	**Baked Rigatoni and**	**Easy Creamy**
Muffins	**Carrots and Raisins**	**Cauliflower**	**Hummus**
1 serving • 169 Cal	1 serving • 432 Cal	1 serving • 406 Cal	1 serving • 266 Cal
(Make leftovers)	(Make leftovers)	**Watermelon Feta and**	**Cucumber**
Strawberries		**Mint Salad**	1 cucumber (8-1/4") •
1 cup • 46 Cal		1 serving • 191 Cal	45 Cal (301 g)

Day 10 - 1505 Calories • 229g Carbs (41g Fiber) •43g Fat • 67g Protein

Breakfast	Lunch	Dinner	Snack
254 Cal	432 Cal	534 Cal	286 Cal
Broccoli Cheddar Egg Muffins	**Freekeh with Chickpeas, Carrots and Raisins**	**One-Pan Mediterranean Shrimp**	**Power-Up Green Smoothies**
1 serving • 169 Cal (From Leftovers)	1 serving • 432 Cal (From Leftovers)	1 serving • 319 Cal	1 serving • 286 Cal
Blueberries 1 cup • 84 Cal		**Cherry Clafoutis** 1 serving • 215 Cal	

Day 11 - 1565 Calories • 220g Carbs (37g Fiber) • 58g Fat • 61g Protein

Breakfast	Lunch	Dinner	Snack
334 Cal	423 Cal	689 Cal	119 Cal
Hearty Muesli with Apples and Raisins	**Navy Bean and Fennel Salad**	**Antipasto and Amaranth Salad**	**Tzatziki**
1 serving • 334 Cal	1 serving • 318 Cal	1 serving • 474 Cal	3 tbsp • 45 Cal (45 g)
	Grapes 1 cup • 104 Cal	**Jeweled Fruit en Papillote** 1 serving • 215 Cal	**Pita bread** 1 pita, small (4" dia) • 74 Cal (28 g)

Day 12 - 1546 Calories • 217 Carbs (33g Fiber) • 49g Fat • 82g Protein

Breakfast	Lunch	Dinner	Snack
368 Cal	468 Cal	424 Cal	286 Cal
Make-Ahead Loaded Veggie Bake	**Chicken, Feta and Kalamata Wraps**	**Delightful Greek Hand Pies**	**Power-Up Green Smoothies**
1 serving • 263 Cal (Make leftovers)	1 serving • 373 Cal	1 serving • 406 Cal	1 serving • 286 Cal
Banana 1 banana • 105 Cal	**Apple** 1 apple • 95 Cal	**Lettuce** 1 cup shredded • 5 Cal **Low-Fat Balsamic Vinaigrette** 1 tbsp • 13 Cal	

Day 13 - 1566 Calories • 180 Carbs (29g Fiber) • 62g Fat • 85g Protein

Breakfast	Lunch	Dinner	Snack
327 Cal	256 Cal	766 Cal	217 Cal
Make-Ahead Loaded Veggie Bake	**Sweet and Savory Basmati Rice Salad**	**Lemon Salmon with Lima Beans**	**Make-It-Your-Own Fruit, Nut and Seed Bars**
1 serving • 263 Cal (From leftovers)	1 serving • 256 Cal	1 serving • 316 Cal	1 serving • 217 CaL
Raspberries 1 cup • 64 Cal (123 g)		**Quinoa** 1/2 cup • 111 Cal **Turkish Yogurt Cake** 1 serving • 340 Cal	

Day 14 - 1595 Calories • 182g Carbs (26g Fiber) • 68g Fat • 70g Protein

Breakfast	Lunch	Dinner	Snack
226 Cal	258 Cal	874 Cal	208 Cal
Steelcut Oatmeal	**Spinach, Tomato and Mushroom Salad**	**Braised Lamb Shanks**	**Dill-Feta Dip**
1 cup • 150 Cal (prepare according to package directions)	1 serving • 258 Cal	1 serving • 522 Cal	2 tablespoons • 28 Cal
		Porcini Mushroom Risotto with Peas	**Apple**
Banana		1 serving • 221 Cal	1 apple • 95 Cal
1 banana • 105 Cal		**Tapioca Pudding**	**Baby carrots**
		1/2 cup • 130 Cal	1 cup • 86 Cal

WEEK 3

Day 15 — 1566 Calories • 171g Carbs (23g Fiber) • 64g Fat • 80g Protein

Breakfast	Lunch	Dinner	Snack
337 Cal	489 Cal	454 Cal	286 Cal
Greek-Inspired Omelet	**Tuscan Baked Ziti**	**Baked Tuna Steaks with Garlic Aioli**	**Power-Up Green Smoothies**
1 serving • 337 Cal	1 serving • 489 Cal (Make leftovers)	1 serving • 371 Cal	1 serving • 286 Cal
		Sweet and Tangy Cucumber Salad	
		1 serving • 82 Cal	

Day 16 - 1562 Calories • 218g Carbs (47g Fiber) • 59g Fat • 56g Protein

Breakfast	Lunch	Dinner	Snack
193 Cal	482 Cal	625 Cal	263 Cal
Overnight Oatmeal with Fruit and Yogurt	**Garlic and Herb Lentil Salad**	**Turkish Stuffed Eggplant**	**Apple Granola and Yogurt Mini Trifle**
1 serving • 193 Cal	1 serving • 417 Cal	1 serving • 404 Cal	1 serving • 263 Cal
	Baby carrots	**Angel Food Cake with Strawberries and Cream**	
	3/4 cup • 65 Cal)	1 serving • 221 Cal	

Day 17 - 1541 Calories • 220g Carbs (31g Fiber) • 41g Fat • 81g Protein

Breakfast	Lunch	Dinner	Snack
246 Cal	489 Cal	614 Cal	192 Cal
Grab 'N Go Fruit Smoothies	**Tuscan Baked Ziti**	**Herb Roasted Sea Bass**	**Cottage cheese**
1 serving • 246 Cal	1 serving • 489 Cal	1 serving • 255 Cal	1/2 cup • 92 Cal
	(From leftovers)	**Simple Lebanese Rice**	**Blueberries**
		1 serving • 171 Cal	1/2 cup • 42 Cal
		Steamed Green Beans with Lemon-Tarragon	**Chia seeds**
		2 servings • 62 Cal	1 tbsp • 58 Cal
		Strawberry Granita	
		1 serving • 126 Cal	
		(Make leftovers)	

Day 18 - 1567 Calories • 177g Carbs (28g Fiber) • 65g Fat • 81g Protein

Breakfast	Lunch	Dinner	Snack
264 Cal	439 Cal	687 Cal	176 Cal
Broccoli Cheddar Egg Muffins	**Chickpea, Zucchini and Tomatoes with Pesto**	**Chicken Souvlaki with Tzatziki Sauce**	**Rice cakes**
1 serving • 169 Cal	1 serving • 439 Cal	1 serving • 344 Cal	1 cake • 35 Cal
Apple		**Brown rice**	**Pear**
1 apple • 95 Cal		1 cup cooked • 216 Cal	1 medium • 101 Cal
		Strawberry Granita	**Reduced Fat Feta Cheese**
		1 serving • 126 Cal	1 serving • 40 Cal
		(From leftovers)	

Day 19 - 1553 Calories • 194g Carbs (38g Fiber) • 54g Fat • 92g Protein

Breakfast	Lunch	Dinner	Snack
298 Cal	390 Cal	592 Cal	273 Cal
Grab 'N Go Fruit Smoothies	**Brussels Sprouts and Chickpea Salad**	**Lemon Garlic Baked Cod**	**Smoked salmon and cottage cheese sandwich**
1 serving • 246 Cal	1 serving • 343 Cal	1 serving • 280 Cal	1 sandwich • 228 Cal
Banana	**Tangerine**	**Roasted Apple, Fennel and Pear Salad**	**Cucumber**
1/2 banana • 53 Cal	1 medium • 47 Cal	1 serving • 186 Cal	1 cucumber • 45 Cal
		Strawberry Granita	
		1 serving • 126 Cal	
		(From leftovers)	

Day 20 - 1641 Calories • 186g Carbs (25g Fiber) • 66g Fat • 81g Protein

Breakfast	Lunch	Dinner	Snack
353 Cal	398 Cal	707 Cal	183 Cal
Whole Grain Bread	**Tuscan-Style Salad with**	**Steamed Mussels with**	**Yogurt with**
2 slices • 228 Cal	**Roasted Peppers and**	**Tomatoes and Olives**	**Blueberries and**
Hass Avocado	**Green Olives**	1 serving • 358 Cal	**Almonds**
1/2 medium • 125 Cal	1 serving • 398 Cal	**French Bread**	1 serving • 183 Cal
		1 slice • 229 Cal	
		Sugar Snap Pea and	
		Radish Salad	
		1 serving • 120 Cal	

Day 21 - 1516 Calories • 156g Carbs (28g Fiber) • 68g Fat • 76g Protein

Breakfast	Lunch	Dinner	Snack
288 Cal	373 Cal	756 Cal	99 Cal
Scrambled Eggs with	**Pasta Primavera**	**Bass with Sweet and**	**Tzatziki Sauce**
Spinach, Tomato and	1 serving • 373 Cal	**Sour Agrodolce Sauce**	1 serving • 50 Cal
Ricotta		1 serving • 433 Cal	**Celery**
1 serving • 209 Cal		**Tabbouleh**	1 stalk • 6 Cal
Cantaloupe		1 serving • 172 Cal	**Baby carrots**
2 slices • 47 Cal		**Gelato (store-bought)**	1/2 cup • 43 Cal
Raspberries		1 serving • 150 Cal	
1/2 cup • 32 Cal			

WEEK 4

Day 22 - 1570 Calories • 189g Carbs (30g Fiber) • 55g Fat • 91g Protein

Breakfast	Lunch	Dinner	Snack
193 Cal	309 Cal	766 Cal	302 Cal
Overnight Oatmeal with	**Roasted Red Pepper**	**Roasted Garlic Dijon**	**Fattoush**
Fruit and Yogurt	**Hummus Tostadas**	**Pork Loin**	1 serving • 172 Cal
1 serving • 193 Cal	1 serving • 301 Cal	1 serving • 284 Cal	**Roasted Sea Salt**
	Tomatoes	**Orzo**	**Chickpeas**
	2 slices • 8 Cal	1/3 cup dry • 210 Cal	**(Store-bought)**
		(Prepare according to	1/3 cup • 130 Cal
		package directions)	
		Roasted Vegetables	
		with Garlic and Thyme	
		1 serving • 146 Cal	
		Strawberry Granita	
		1 serving • 126 Cal	
		(From leftovers)	

Day 23 - 1517 Calories • 189g Carbs (29g Fiber) • 57g Fat • 71g Protein

Breakfast	Lunch	Dinner	Snack
298 Cal	557 Cal	491 Cal	171 Cal
Grab 'N Go Fruit Smoothies	Panzanella with Cucumbers and Cherry Tomatoes	Moroccan Root Vegetable Tagine	Plain Greek Yogurt 3/4 cup • 97 Cal
1 serving • 246 Cal	1 serving • 484 Cal	1 serving • 212 Cal	Blueberries
Banana	Tuna, flaked	Moroccan Carrot Salad	1/2 cup • 42 Cal
1/2 banana • 53 Cal	(Packed in water)	1 serving • 279 Cal	Blackberries
	3 oz • 73 Cal		1/2 cup • 31 Cal
	(Sprinkle over salad)		

Day 24 - 1556 Calories • 212g Carbs (37g Fiber) • 66g Fat • 54g Protein

Breakfast	Lunch	Dinner	Snack
152 Cal	526 Cal	610 Cal	268 Cal
Eggs	Chickpea, Zucchini and Tomatoes with Pesto	Whole Grain Lasagna with Eggplant and Olives	Healthy Trail mix (Store-bought)
1 egg • 70 Cal	1 serving • 439 Cal	1 serving • 324 Cal	1/4 cup • 173 Cal
Grapefruit	Sweet cherries	(Make leftovers)	Apple
1 medium • 82 Cal	1 cup, with pits • 87 Cal	Berries and Honey Ginger Yogurt	1 apple • 95 Cal
		1 serving • 286 Cal	

Day 25 - 1547 Calories • 179g Carbs (34g Fiber) • 67g Fat • 68g Protein

Breakfast	Lunch	Dinner	Snack
286 Cal	324 Cal	585 Cal	351 Cal
Quinoa and Feta Egg Muffins	Whole Grain Lasagna with Eggplant and Olives	Chicken Artichoke and Tomato Casserole	Peanut butter 2 tbsp • 191 Cal
2 muffins • 225 Cal	1 serving • 324 Cal	1 serving • 287 Cal	Baby carrots
Oranges	(From leftovers)	Brown rice	1/2 cup • 43 Cal
1 orange • 62 Cal		2/3 cup • 144 Cal	Celery
		(cook according to package directions)	2 stalks • 13 Cal
		Grilled Asparagus	Grapes
		1 serving • 53 Cal	1 cup • 104 Cal
		Dried Figs with Ricotta and Walnuts	
		1 serving • 101 Cal	

Day 26 - 1563 Calories • 211g Carbs (30g Fiber) • 55g Fat • 66g Protein

Breakfast	Lunch	Dinner	Snack
285 Cal	354 Cal	707 Cal	217 Cal
Steelcut Oatmeal	**Clementines**	**Salmon with Sun-Dried Tomato Couscous**	**Make-It-Your-Own Fruit, Nut and Seed Bars**
1 serving • 150 Cal (Prepare according to package directions using)	2 Clementines • 80 Cal	1 serving • 524 Cal	1 serving • 217 Cal (Make leftovers)
Almond milk	**Dried Apricots**	**Spinach**	
1/2 cup • 30 Cal	6 Pieces • 120 Cal	3 cups • 21 Cal	
Banana	**Plain Yogurt**	**Strawberries**	
1 medium • 105 Cal	1 cup (8 fl oz) • 154 Cal	1 cup sliced • 53 Cal	
		Strawberry Vinaigrette	
		2 tbsp • 110 Cal	

Day 27 - 1542 Calories • 194g Carbs (31g Fiber) • 61g Fat • 71g Protein

Breakfast	Lunch	Dinner	Snack
295 Cal	386 Cal	645 Cal	217 Cal
Mango Coconut Green Smoothie	**Tuna, Green Beans and Tomatoes with Shells**	**Marinated Shrimp and Vegetable Kabobs**	**Make-It-Your-Own Fruit, Nut and Seed Bars**
1 serving • 295 Cal	1 serving • 386 Cal	1 serving • 285 Cal	1 serving • 217 Cal (From leftovers)
		Cantaloupe and Raspberries with Tarragon and Mint	
		1 serving • 217 Cal	
		Tapioca pudding	
		4 oz • 143 Cal	

Day 28 - 1546 Calories • 214g Carbs (36g Fiber) • 62g Fat • 53g Protein

Breakfast	Lunch	Dinner	Snack
391 Cal	191 Cal	640 Cal	324 Cal
Power-Up Green Smoothie	**Watermelon Feta and Mint Salad**	**Mediterranean Stuffed Chicken**	**Fruit Cup Chia Pudding**
1 serving • 286 Cal	1 serving • 191 Cal	1 serving • 393 Cal	1 serving • 324 Cal
Banana		**Sugar Snap Pea and Radish Salad**	
1 banana • 105 Cal		1 serving • 120 Cal	
		Strawberry Granita	
		1 serving • 126 Cal	

BREAKFAST
AND SNACKS

Asparagus and Mushroom Frittata

This delicious frittata is very special way to start your day and save your leftovers for lunch. You can prepare this dish ahead of time to make your morning easier.

Makes 4 Servings

Calories 326 | Carbohydrate 14 g | Fiber 3 g | Fat 19 g | Protein 26 g

3 eggs
2 egg whites
1 cup parmesan cheese
1/2 cup fresh basil
  leaves, torn
Kosher salt and freshly
  ground pepper
1 tbsp virgin olive oil
1 leek, sliced
1 lb asparagus, trimmed
  and cut into 1-inch
  pieces
8 oz sliced baby Bella
  mushrooms
1 cup shredded part
  skim mozzarella

Tips
* Rinse leeks well to remove any dirt. Pat dry with a paper towel.
* The frittata can be covered and refrigerated for up to 5 days.

1. Preheat oven to 400°F.
2. In a large bowl, whisk eggs and egg whites. Stir in parmesan cheese and basil. Season with salt and pepper. Set aside.
3. In a large nonstick skillet over medium heat, add oil and heat until shimmering. Add leeks and cook, stirring occasionally, 3 minutes or until starting to soften. Add asparagus and mushrooms; cook, stirring occasionally, 5 to 7 minutes or until asparagus and mushrooms have softened and mushrooms have released most of their moisture.
4. Pour egg mixture into skillet. Using a nonstick spatula, cook eggs, gently pull eggs across the pan, 2 minutes or until just beginning to set on the bottom. Sprinkle mozzarella cheese over the top.
5. Bake 10 to 12 minutes or until center is set.
6. Using your spatula, loosen edges and slide out onto serving plate to serve immediately.

Easy Crustless Market Vegetable Quiche

Served with eggs for healthy protein, lots of healthy vegetables, and a slice of whole grain toast, you.will have conquered the base of the Mediterranean Diet Pyramid. You can substitute your favorite vegetables and enjoy for breakfast, lunch, or dinner.

Makes 6 Servings

Calories 230 | Carbohydrate 6 g | Fiber 1 g | Fat 16 g | Protein 16 g

2 tbsp virgin olive oil
1 large onion, cut in half lengthwise and sliced into half circles
Kosher salt
2 cups lightly packed spinach
1 yellow squash or zucchini, sliced
1 tomato, seeded and chopped
1 tbsp fresh rosemary leaves
8 large eggs
1 cup milk
1 cup grated sharp cheddar or Monterey Jack
Freshly ground black pepper

Tips
* You can substitute steamed cauliflower and broccoli florets for the squash and zucchini,

1. Preheat oven to 400°F.
2. In a large skillet over medium heat, add 1 tbsp oil and heat until shimmering. Add the onion, season with salt and cook, stirring occasionally, 10 to 15 minutes or until onion is softened and lightly browned. Arrange onions over the bottom of a deep dish glass pie pan. Set aside.
3. Add remaining oil to the skillet and heat until shimmering. Add the spinach, squash and tomatoes; cook, stirring occasionally, 3 to 5 minutes or until spinach is wilted and vegetables are softened. Stir in rosemary. Transfer vegetables to pie pan and arrange evenly on top of onions.
4. In a medium bowl, gently beat eggs. Mix in the milk, cheese and 1 tsp salt and 1/2 tsp pepper. Pour mixture over the vegetables.
5. Bake 45 minutes or until the surface is lightly brown and a knife inserted in the center comes out clean.
6. Let quiche stand 20 minutes to cool. To serve, slice into wedges.

Greek-Inspired Omelet

With flavors reminiscent of the classic Greek spanakopita, this easy omelet is just right for breakfast, lunch or a light dinner accompanied by a bowl of fruit or berries.

Makes 1 Serving

Calories 337 | Carbohydrate 5 g | Fiber 2 g | Fat 27 g | Protein 18 g

2 large eggs
2 tbsp water
Kosher salt
Freshly ground black
   pepper
1 tbsp butter
1/4 cup chopped baby
   spinach
2 green onions, thinly
   sliced
3 tbsp crumbled feta
   cheese
1 tbsp chopped fresh dill
Freshly ground pepper

1. In a medium bowl, gently beat eggs, water, 1/4 tsp salt and a pinch of pepper.
2. In a medium nonstick skillet over medium-high heat, add the butter and heat until melted, tilting and turning pan to coat the bottom.
3. Pour in egg mixture. When eggs set at edges, use an inverted silicone spatula to gently push cooked eggs from the edges to the middle, allowing uncooked eggs to move to the hot parts of the pan. Continue cooking and pushing until no visible liquid remains.
4. Arrange spinach, onions and feta on one side of the omelet. Sprinkle with dill. Using the spatula, fold omelet in half. Slide or invert omelet onto a serving plate.
5. Serve immediately. Season to taste with salt and pepper.

Make-Ahead Loaded Veggie Bake

Cook up a very healthy meal using mushrooms, carrots, bell peppers, onions, potatoes and dark leafy greens, topped with cheese, smothered in eggs, and baked to perfection.

Makes 8 Servings

Calories 263 | Carbohydrate 20 g | Fiber 3 g | Fat 11 g | Protein 22 g

2 tbsp virgin olive oil
2 cloves garlic, minced
8 oz sliced button mushrooms
2 cups shredded carrots
1 cup frozen diced bell pepper and onion mix
4 cups firmly packed baby kale, torn into bite-size pieces
2 cups frozen diced potatoes
2 cups fat free shredded sharp cheddar cheese
12 large eggs
2 cups reduced fat (2%) milk
Kosher salt
Freshly ground black pepper
1 tsp fresh thyme leaves

1. Preheat oven to 375°F.
2. Grease a 9-by 13-inch baking dish with 1 tbsp oil. Set aside.
3. In a large skillet over medium heat, add oil and heat until shimmering. Add the mushrooms, carrots and bell pepper mix; cook, stirring occasionally, about 5 to 7 minutes or until tender. Add the kale and cook, tossing often, 5 minutes or until softened and liquids are evaporated. Stir in potatoes. Transfer to the prepared baking dish and spread evenly on the bottom of the dish. Sprinkle vegetables with cheese.
4. In a large bowl, whisk the egg, milk, 2 tsp salt, 1/4 tsp pepper and the thyme. Pour over the vegetables.
5. Bake 40 to 50 minutes or until the top is golden brown and a knife inserted in the middle comes out clean. Let cool for 10 minutes before cutting.
6. Serve immediately or cover and refrigerate individual serving pieces for up to 5 days. Servings can also be tightly covered and frozen for up to 3 months.

Tips
* Prepare the dish through step 4. Cover and refrigerate overnight. Continue with step 5, increasing the baking time by 5 to 10 minutes.

Shakshuka

An easy to prepare shakshuka recipe of eggs braised in a perfectly spiced sauce of fresh tomatoes and peppers.

Makes 6 Servings

Calories 414 | Carbohydrate 47 g | Fiber 5g | Fat 19 g | Protein 14 g

3 tbsp virgin olive oil
2 green bell peppers, cored, seeded and chopped
1 large yellow onion, chopped
2 cloves garlic, finely chopped
1 tsp ground coriander
1 tsp paprika
1⁄2 tsp ground cumin
Pinch red pepper flakes
Kosher salt
6 tomatoes, chopped
1⁄2 cup tomato sauce
1 tsp sugar
6 large eggs
1⁄4 cup chopped fresh parsley leaves
1⁄4 cup chopped fresh mint leaves
6 slices thick crusty bread warmed

1. In a large heavy bottom skillet over medium heat, add the oil and heat until shimmering. Add the bell pepper and onion; cook, stirring often, 5 to 7 minutes of until the vegetables are softened. Add the garlic, coriander, paprika, cumin, pepper flakes and a pinch of salt; cook, stirring, 1 minute or until the garlic is fragrant.
2. Add the tomatoes, tomatoe sauce and sugar; cook, stirring occasionally, 10 minutes or until the mixture starts to reduce and thicken.
3. Using the back of a spoon, make 6 indentations, spaced apart, in the tomato mixture. Carefully crack and egg into each indentation.
4. Reduce the heat to medium-low and cook, covered, until the egg whites are opaque and eggs are done to your liking. Sprinkle with parsely and mint. Season to taste with salt and pepper.
5. Ladle eggs and sauce onto individual serving plates. Serve with warm crusty bread.

Scrambled Eggs with Spinach, Tomato and Ricotta

In as little as 5 minutes you can prepare these delicious Mediterranean scrambled eggs with spinach, tomato and creamy ricotta that are bursting with the nutrients needed to give your day a healthy start.

Makes 2 Servings

Calories 209 | Carbohydrate 4 g | Fiber 1 g | Fat 15 g | Protein 14 g

1 tbsp virgin olive oil
1 Roma tomato, seeded
  and diced
1 cup lightly packed
  baby spinach
3 eggs
1 egg white (optional)
Kosher salt
2 tbsp part skim ricotta
  cheese
Freshly ground black
  pepper

1. In a small bowl, add the eggs, egg white (if using) and a pinch of salt. Using a fork, gently beat the eggs.
2. In a medium skillet over medium heat, add the oil and heat until shimmering. Add the tomatoes and spinach; cook, stirring often, 3 minutes or until the spinach is wilted.
3. Add the eggs to the spinach mixture and cook, gently folding, 30 second and then add the ricotta. Continue cooking and folding egg mixture, until egg whites are opaque and eggs are done to your like.
4. Transfer serving plates. Season to taste with salt and pepper.

Broccoli Cheddar Egg Muffins

These delicious muffins can easily be made ahead of time and become a perfect grab and run treat for people on-the-go.

Makes 6 Servings

Calories 169 | Carbohydrate 4 g | Fiber 2 g | Fat 10 g | Protein 17 g

8 eggs
4 egg whites
1/2 tbsp Dijon mustard
Kosher salt
Freshly ground black
    pepper
2 cups frozen chopped
    broccoli, thawed
3/4 cup reduced fat
    shredded cheddar
    cheese
2 green onions, sliced
1/4 cup milk

1. Preheat oven to 350°F.
2. Spray a standard muffin tin with nonstick cooking spray. Set aside.
3 In a large bowl, whisk the eggs, egg whites, mustard, 2 tsp salt and 1/2 tsp pepper. Stir in the broccoli, cheese, onions and milk. Pour the mixture into the muffin tin.
4. Bake 12 to 14 minutes until a knife inserted in the center comes out clean and the egg are slightly puffed.

Variation
*   *Broccoli and Bacon:* Replace the broccoli with 6 tbsp crumbled cooked bacon and 1 diced zucchini. Replace the cheddar cheese with mozzarella.

Quinoa and Feta Egg Muffins

These nutrient and protein packed muffins are enriched with Mediterranean vegetables, herbs and spices that will make your to-go breakfast or lunch a satisfying and healthy choice.

Makes 12 Muffins (2 muffins per serving)

Calories 225 | Carbohydrate 13 g | Fiber 3 g | Fat 13 g | Protein 16 g

4 tsp virgin olive oil (approx.)
½ cup finely chopped onion
1 cup chopped tomatoes
2 cups baby spinach (finely chopped)
½ cup chopped kalamata olives
1 tbsp chopped fresh oregano
8 eggs
1 cup cooked quinoa
1 cup crumbled feta cheese
Kosher salt
¼ teaspoon salt

1. Preheat oven to 350°F.
2. Grease a 12 cup muffin tin with about 2 tsp oil. Set aside.
3. In a large skillet over medium heat, add 2 tsp oil and heat until shimmering. Add the onions and cook, stirring often, 3 minutes. Add the tomatoes and the spinach and cook, tossing, 2 minutes or until vegetables are softened and spinach is wilted. Remove from heat. Stir in olives and oregano. Set aside.
4. In a large bowl, whisk eggs. Stir in quinoa, feta vegetable mixture and 1 tsp salt.
5. Pour mixture into muffin tins and bake, 30 minutes or until muffins are golden and a knife inserted into the center of a muffin comes out clean. Let stand 7 minutes to cool.
6. Serve immediately or cover tightly and refrigerate up to 5 days.

Roasted Red Pepper Hummus Tostadas

This riff on a popular Mexican dish will give you a healthy kick start to your day with a perfect balance of nutrients from eggs, hummus, tomatoes, and avocados.

Makes 4 Servings

Calories 301 | Carbohydrate 19 g | Fiber 3 g | Fat 18 g | Protein 17 g

4 corn tortillas (6-in diameter)
Grapeseed oil
6 eggs
1/2 cup diced tomatoes, divided
1/3 cup sliced green onions, divided
1/2 tsp ground cumin
1/2 tsp garlic powder
1/4 tsp Kosher salt
Nonstick cooking spray
Water
1 cup shredded Swiss cheese
1/2 cup roasted red pepper hummus
1 avocado, peeled, pitted and sliced

1. Preheat oven to 425°F.
2. Brush both sides of tortillas with oil and place on a baking sheet. Bake 8 minutes or until crisp. Set aside.
3. In a medium bowl, beat eggs. Stir in 1/4 cup tomatoes, 3 tbsp onions, cumin, garlic powder and salt.
4. In a large skillet over medium heat, add butter and heat until melted, tilting pan to coat the bottom. Add egg mixture and cook, stirring often, 3 minutes or until eggs are set and soft.
5. Remove from heat and stir in 3/4 cup cheese.
6. Transfer tortillas to serving plates and spread with hummus. Evenly divide egg mixture among tortillas. Sprinkle with remaining tomatoes, cheese and green onions.
7. Serve topped avocado slices.

Overnight Oatmeal with Fruit and Yogurt

An easy to prepare, make-ahead breakfast or snack packed with-powerhouse nutrients for busy people on the go.

Makes 1 Serving

Calories 193 | Carbohydrate 31 g | Fiber 6 g | Fat 3 g | Protein 12 g

1/2 cup rolled (old-fashion) oats
1/2 cup skim milk
1/2 cup fat free plain Greek yogurt
1 tsp chia seeds
1/2 cup blueberries
1/2 cup strawberries, cored and chopped

1. In an 8 oz canning jar add oatmeal and pour in milk. Layer yogurt, chia seeds, blueberries and strawberries.
2. Cover and refrigerate 8 hours or overnight.
3. Serve chilled.

Note: Overnight oats can be covered tightly and refrigerated for up to 5 days.

Hearty Muesli with Apples and Raisins

This tasty crunchy muesli is packed with heart-healthy rolled oats, walnuts, and sunflower seeds. Muesli is an ideal make-ahead dish that can be enjoyed for several days.

Makes 14 Servings

Calories 334 | Carbohydrate 40 g | Fiber 6 g | Fat 17 g | Protein 11 g

4 cups rolled (old-fashion) oats
2 cups walnuts, coarsely chopped
1 cup sunflower seeds
1 tbsp virgin olive oil
1/2 tsp Kosher salt
1/4 tsp ground cinnamon
1 cup dried apple pieces
1/2 cup raisins

1. Preheat oven to 350°F.
2. In a large bowl, combine the oats, walnuts, sunflower seeds, oil, salt and cinnamon. On a baking sheet, spread mixture in a thin layer. Bake 5 minutes or until fragrant and light golden. Let cool. Stir in dried apples and raisins. Cover tightly and store at room temperature for up to 2 weeks.

Suggested Toppings: Chopped fresh apple, fat free Greek yogurt (1/2 cup per serving), honey.

Make-It-Your-Own Fruit, Nut and Seed Bars

This mix-and-match crunchy bar is packed with nutrients and can be made with a variety of ingredients to suit your tastes. Use up nuts, seeds or dried fruits from your pantry for an even more economical bar.

Makes 18 Bars

Calories 217 | Carbohydrate 31 g | Fiber 5 g | Fat 10 g | Protein 4 g

2 cups old-fashioned rolled oats

1 cup nuts (for example almonds, pecans, walnuts or pistachios)

1-1/2 cups dried fruits, (for example cranberries, cherries, raisins or dates)

1/2 cup honey

1/4 tsp Kosher salt

1/2 cup unsweetened shredded coconut

1/2 cup seeds (for example pumpkin, sunflower, sesame or flax)

1 tbsp butter

1. Preheat oven to 425°F.
2. Arrange oats and nuts on a rimmed baking sheet. Bake 7 minutes or until nicely toasted. Let cool slightly.
3. Transfer mixture to a food processor. Add dried fruits, honey and salt; pulse to combine, leaving some pieces coarsely chopped.
4. Add coconut and seed; pulsing to combine.
5. Spray a 9-by 14-inch baking pan with nonstick cooking spray. Line pan with foil and coat with butter. Press mixture firmly into the pan.
6. Bake 20 minutes or until browned and firm. Cool completely.
7. Using the edges of the foil, remove bars from pan. Using a serrated knife, cut into bars.
8. Bars can be stored in an airtight container, separated by parchment paper, up to 2 weeks.

*Per serving nutritional values are estimated because of the variety of ingredients that can be added or substituted.

Grab 'N Go Fruit Smoothies

A smoothie is one of those sure fire ways to get you the right nutrients and the boost you need at anytime of the day.

Makes 1 Serving

Calories 246 | Carbohydrate 44 g | Fiber 8 g | Fat 4 g | Protein 11 g

1 frozen banana, halved
1 cup frozen blueberries
2/3 cup fat free plain
    Greek yogurt
1/2 cup old-fashioned
    rolled oats
1 tbsp ground flax seeds
2 tsp lemon juice
1 tsp pure vanilla extract

1. Add banana, blueberries, yogurt, oats, flax seeds, lemon juice, vanilla and 1/3 cup water to a blender. Cover and blend for 1 minute. Add more water, if needed, and blend until your desired consistency is reached.

Power-Up Green Smoothies

Makes 1 Serving

Calories 286 | Carbohydrate 69 g | Fiber 13 g | Fat 2 g | Protein 6 g

1 cup baby kale
1 banana
3/4 cup cranberries
3/4 cup blueberries
3 ice cubes
1 cup coconut water
1/2 tbsp pomegranate
    powder (optional)

1. Add kale, banana, cranberries, blueberries, ice cubes, coconut water, and pomegranate power (if using) to a blender. Cover and blend for 1 minute. Add more water, if needed, and blend until your desired consistency is reached.

Tip If using frozen berries, reduce or omit the ice cubes.

> **Variation**
> * *Mango Coconut Green Smoothie* (295 Calories): Replace the berries with 1-1/2 cups mango cubes. Garnish with unsweetened shredded coconut if desired.

Blueberry Yogurt Parfait

This little gem of a dish is healthy, colorful and perfect for breakfast, a snack, or dessert.

Makes 1 Serving

Calories 232 | Carbohydrate 35 g | Fiber 5 g | Fat 2 g | Protein 20 g

3/4 cup plain fat free
  Greek yogurt,
  divided
1/3 cup blueberries
1/3 cup natural granola
  with raisins

1. In a serving bowls, layer half of the yogurt, the granola, the remaining yogurt and the blueberries.

> Variation:
> ***Yogurt with Blueberries and Almonds*** (183 Calories): Increase blueberries to 1/2 cup. Replace granola with 5 sliced almonds. 183 Cal

Feta Dill Dip

This refreshing dip is so versatile, you will find yourself making it again-and-again. It is perfect as an appetizer with carrots, celery and other veggie dipppers or as lovely snack.

Makes About 1-1/2 Cups

Calories 28 | Carbohydrate 3 g | Fiber 0 g | Fat 2 g | Protein 1 g

1 cup plain full-fat Greek
  yogurt
3 oz feta cheese
1 medium clove garlic,
  halved
1 tbsp fresh lemon juice
2 tbsp chopped dill
1-1/2 tsp grated lemon
  zest
Kosher salt
Freshly ground black
  pepper

1. In a food processor, add the yogurt, cheese, garlic, lemon juice, lemon zest and dill. Process until almost smooth. Season to taste with salt and pepper. Let stand for 30 minutes. Serve.

> Tip
> *   Dip can be covered tightly and refrigerated for up to 1 week.

Easy Creamy Hummus

There is nothing quite like the depth of flavor and creaminess from homemade hummus. This recipe uses dried chickpeas for ideal flavor and texture, but you can substitute canned. Serve it with vegetables, pita wedges or flatbread.

Makes 4 Cups

Calories 266 | Carbohydrate 32 g | Fiber 10 g | Fat 13 g | Protein 11 g

1-1/2 cups dried chickpeas, rinsed and drained
1 tsp baking soda
7 cups water
1/4 cup fresh lemon juice
1⁄4 cup tahini
3 tbsp extra virgin olive oil (approx.)
1 clove garlic, minced
1/2 tsp ground cumin
3 tbsp water (approx.)
Kosher salt
Ground paprika

> **Tip**
> * Hummus can be covered and refrigerated for up to 4 days.
> * If using canned chickpeas, you will need about 1-1/2 15 oz cans.
> * Garnish with fresh pomegranate seeds or black olives

1. In a large bowl, combine chickpeas and 6 cups cold water. Let stand at room temperature 8 hours or overnight. Drain and rinse.
2. In a large stockpot over high heat, add the chickpeas and baking soda; cook, stirring, 3 minutes. Add the water and heat until boiling. Reduce heat to simmering and cook, skimming off any foam or skins, 10 to 40 minutes or until tender, checking doneness every 5 minutes after the first 10 minutes. Drain and rinse.
3. In a food processor, add the tahini and lemon juice; process, scraping down the sides, for 90 seconds or until creamy. Add 2 tbsp oil, the garlic, cumin and 1/2 tsp salt; process, scraping the sides, 1 minute or until blended.
4. Add half of the chickpeas and process, scraping the sides, for 1 minute. Add the remaining chickpeas and process, scraping the sides, 2 minutes or until smooth. Add water, 1 tbsp at a time, and process until desired consistency.
5. Transfer to a serving bowl. Season to taste with salt. Using the back of a spoon, make a swirled indentation on top of the hummus and drizzle with oil. Serve garnished with paprika.

Baba Ghanouj

This classic Middle Eastern dip is made with roasted eggplant, tahini, lemon juice, yogurt, and infused with garlic. Serve with fresh vegetables and pita bread for dipping for a fabulous treat.

Makes About 2 Cups

Calories 240 | Carbohydrate 32 g | Fiber 15 g | Fat 12 g | Protein 7 g

2 lbs eggplant (about 2 Globe or 4 Italian), halved lengthwise
Kosher salt
Extra virgin olive oil
1/4 freshly lemon juice (approx.)
1/4 cup tahini, stirred well
2 tbsp plain yogurt
2 cloves garlic, halved
Chopped parsley leaves

Tip
* Baba Ghanouj can be prepared several hours ahead of time. Do not store overnight as the ingredients meld and become more pungent.

1. Using a sharp knife, score the flesh deeply in a cross-hatch pattern. Press on the eggplant to open the cuts and sprinkle with 1-1/2 tsp salt. Set aside, cut side up, for 30 minutes.
2. Preheat oven to 400°F.
3. Line a baking sheet with parchment.
4. Squeeze the juice from the eggplants and discard. Using a paper towel, wipe eggplant dry. Brush cut sides completely with oil. On a parchment-lined baking sheet, arrange eggplant cut side down.
5. Bake 1 hour or until the eggplants collapse and the flesh-side is a deep brown caramel color. Transfer eggplant to a colander over a sink and let cool 20 minutes. Using a spoon, scoop out flesh and let stand in the colander 30 minutes or until room temperature. Discard stems and skin.
6. Meanwhile using a mortar and pestle, mash garlic with a generous pinch of salt into a paste. Transfer paste to a food processor.
7. Add the eggplant, lemon juice, tahini and yogurt; puree mixture.
8. Transfer to a bowl. Drizzle with olive oil. Serve garnished with parsley.

SALADS AND SIDES

Classic Greek Salad

This classic Greek salad is the epitome of the how fresh vegetables, olives, cheese, herbs, and a tasty light vinaigrette can make the perfect side dish or just as satisfying as a main dish. Make it as a side salad and save any leftovers for lunch.

Makes 4 Servings

Calories 323 | Carbohydrate 23 g | Fiber 5 g | Fat 24 g | Protein 8 g

1/4 cup red wine vinegar

1 lemon, zest and juice of

1 tsp dried oregano

1 tsp honey

Kosher salt

Freshly ground black pepper

1/4 cup extra-virgin olive oi

5 Persian cucumbers, halved lengthwise and cut crosswise into 1/2-inch slices

12 small roma tomatoes, cut into 2-inch chunks

1 cup pitted kalamata olives, halved

1 small red onion, chopped

4 oz feta cheese cubes packed in brine

1. In a large bowl, whisk the vinegar, lemon zest, lemon juice, oregano, honey 1 tsp salt and 1/4 tsp pepper. Slowly whisk in the olive oil until emulsified.
2. Add the cucumbers, tomatoes, olives and red onion to the vinaigrette; tossing to combine. Let stand for 15 minutes to meld flavors.
3. Spoon salad on to serving plates and serve sprinkled with feta cubes.

Tuscan-Style Salad with Roasted Peppers and Green Olives

This salad emphasises why a bread salad could be called the coat-of-many-colors with the multitude of ingredient variations. This fantastic version takes fresh roasted bell peppers, green onions and of course large bread cubes for an inviting and colorful salad.

Makes 6 Servings

Calories 398 | Carbohydrate 42 g | Fiber 3 g | Fat 22 g | Protein 7 g

1 red bell pepper
1 yellow bell pepper
1 lb Italian bread
1/2 cup extra-virgin olive oil
1/4 cup cider vinegar
1 small red onion, quartered and thinly sliced
3 tbsp sliced green olives
1 tbsp minced fresh oregano leaves
Kosher salt
Freshly ground black pepper

Tip
* If salad is too dry befor e serving, drizzle salad with 1 tbsp water at a time until salad is your desired consistency.

1. Preheat oven to 475°F.
2. Line a baking sheet with foil and spray with nonstick cooking spray. Arrange peppers on their side. Bake, turning once, 40 minutes or until peppers are charred, softened and slightly collapsed. Transfer peppers to a paper bag and seal bag tightly. Set aside for 15 minutes.
3. Meanwhile, remove crusts from the bread. Discard crusts or save for another use. Cut bread into 1-inch cubes.
4. Transfer peppers to a cutting board. Remove the stem. Cut peppers in half and remove the seeds and ribs. Cut peppers into 1/4-inch wide slices.
5. In a large bowl, combine roasted peppers and bread cubes. Set aside.
6. In a medium bowl, whisk together oil, vinegar, onions, olives and oregano. Season with salt and pepper. Pour dressing over bread and pepper mixture, tossing well. Let stand 10 minutes. Serve immediately or cover tightly and set aside for up to 2 hours.

Panzanella with Cucumbers and Cherry Tomatoes

This classic bread salad is a much-loved salad across the cool blue seas of the Mediterranean and rightly so. It is light and refreshing with crusty bread cubes and a flavorful vinaigrette.

Makes 6 Servings

Calories 484 | Carbohydrate 53 g | Fiber 4 g | Fat 26 g | Protein 11 g

2 lbs tomatoes, cut into 1-inch pieces

2 cucumbers, peeled and seeded, 1/2-inch pieces

Kosher salt

1 lb sourdough bread, crusts removed and cut into 1-1/2 inch cubes

2/3 cup extra-virgin olive oil, divided

1 shallot, minced

2 cloves garlic, minced

1/2 tsp Dijon mustard

2 tbsp white wine vinegar

1/2 cup lightly packed basil leaves, coarsely chopped

Freshly ground black pepper

1. Preheat oven to 375°F.
2. Place tomatoes and cucumbers in a colander set over a bowl. Sprinkle with 2 tsp salt, tossing to combine. Let drain about 15 to 30 minutes. Discard all but 1/4 cup juice and set aside.
3. In a large bowl, add bread cubes and 2 tbsp oil, tossing to coat bread. Transfer bread to a baking sheet. Bake 15 to 20 minutes or until crisp but not browned. Let cool.
4. In the bowl with the juice, add shallot, garlic, mustard and vinegar. Whisking constantly, drizzle in remaining oil. Season to taste with salt and pepper.
5. In a large bowl, combine tomato and cucumber mixture, bread cubes and basil. Drizzle in vinaigrette, tossing to coat. Let stand 30 minutes, tossing occasionally, until dressing is absorbed and flavors are melded.

Kale with Raisins and Pine Nuts

Toasted pine nuts and sweet raisins complete this healthy kale salad that is married with a sweet balsamic vinaigrette.

Makes 6 Servings

Calories 209 | Carbohydrate 28 g | Fiber 4 g | Fat 10 g | Protein 7 g

1/4 cup golden raisins
1/4 cup hot water
2 tbsp pine nuts
3 tbsp virgin olive oil
3 lbs baby kale, stemmed
1 small red onion, thinly sliced
1/4 cup balsamic vinegar
1 tsp lightly packed brown sugar
Kosher salt

1. In a small bowl, add raisins and cover with hot water.
2. In a Dutch oven over medium heat, add the pine nuts and toast, stirring often, 5 minutes or until golden. Transfer to a plate and set aside
3. Increase heat to high. Add 1 tbsp oil to the same Dutch oven and heat until shimmering. Add kale, in small batches and cook, stirring, until slightly softened before adding the next batch. Cook, stirring, 1 minute or until kale is evenly wilted and glossy.
4. Using tongs, transfer kale to colander in a sink. Press down on kale to release any liquids.
5. Using paper towels, wipe out Dutch oven and reduce heat to medium. Add remaining oil and cook until shimmering. Add the red onion and cook, stirring, 3 to 5 minutes or until softened. Drain raisins an add to shallots. Stir in vinegar and sugar; cook, stirring, 2 minutes or until a syrup. Add spinach and toss to coat. Season to taste with salt.
6. Serve garnished with toasted pine nuts.

Fattoush

A Lebanese staple, this refreshing combination of lettuce, tomatoes, cucumbers, and toasted pita bread chunks is drizzled with a lemony vinaigrette. Adding to the mouthwatering appeal is sprinkles of ground sumac, an abundant regional berry.

Makes 6 to 8 Servings

Calories 129 | Carbohydrate 16 g | Fiber 3 g | Fat 7 g | Protein 3 g

2 6-inch pitas, split
3 tbsp extra-virgin olive oil, divided
1 1/4 tsp ground sumac, divided
1/4 cup lemon juice
Kosher salt
Freshly ground black pepper
1 large head romaine lettuce, coarsely chopped
2 large tomatoes diced
1 large cucumber, peeled, seeded and diced
1/2 thinly sliced red onion
1/3 cup chopped fresh mint

1. Preheat oven to 350°F.
2. Arrange pita halves cut-side up on a baking sheet. Brush with 1 tbsp oil. Sprinkle with 1 tsp sumac. Bake, 15 minutes or until pitas are golden and crisp. Let cool. Break into bite-size pieces.
3. In a large bowl, combine the lettuce, tomatoes, cucumbers, onion, mint, the remaining sumac and the pita pieces.
4. In a small bowl, whisk juice, 1/2 tsp salt, 1/4 tsp pepper. Slowly whisk in remaining oil. Drizzle over lettuce mixture, tossing to coat. Let stand 15 minutes.
5. Season to taste with salt and pepper. Tossing again before serving.

Shepherds Salad

This lovely salad originates in Turkey and is representative of the abundant herbs and unique spices that Turkish markets are famous for.

Makes 6 Servings

Calories 242 | Carbohydrate 12 g | Fiber 4 g | Fat 21 g | Protein 4 g

Citrus Vinaigrette
1/2 small shallot, quartered
1 orange, zest and juice
1 lemon
2 tsp Dijon mustard
1/4 cup extra-virgin olive oil
1/4 cup avocado oil
Freshly ground black pepper
Kosher salt

Salad
1 lb tomatoes, diced
3 small cucumbers, diced
1 green bell pepper, stemmed, seeded and diced
1/2 small red onion, finely chopped
1/4 cup loosely packed chopped parsley
1 tbsp chopped dill
2 tbsp chopped mint
1 tsp sumac
4 cups loosely packed spinach
1/2 cup crumbled feta cheese (about 4 oz)

1. *Citrus Vinaigrette:* In a blender, combine the shallot, 1 tsp orange zest, 1/4 cup orange juice, 2 tbsp lemon juice, mustard and Combine shallot, orange zest, orange juice, lemon juice, mustard, 1/2 tsp salt and 1/4 tsp pepper. Slowly oils and blend until smooth.

2. *Salad:* In a large bowl, combine tomatoes, cucumbers, bell pepper, onion, parsley, dill, mint and sumac. Drizzle 1/2 cup of the vinaigrette over the mixture, tossing well. Refrigerate for 30 minutes.

3. Add the spinach and feta, tossing well. Season to taste with salt and pepper. Add more vinaigrette to taste. Serve salad with remaining vinaigrette in a salad dressing bottle.

> Tip
> *   Leftover vinaigrette can be covered and refrigerated for up to 3 days.

SALADS AND SIDES

Sweet and Tangy Cucumber Salad

Makes 4 Servings

Calories 82 | Carbohydrate 18 g | Fiber 2 g | Fat 0 g | Protein 1 g

4 cucumbers, peeled
   and thinly sliced
1 small onion, thinly
   sliced
Kosher salt
1/4 cup granulated
   sugar
1/4 cup white vinegar
1/4 cup water

1. In a medium bowl, add cucumbers and onions. Season generously with salt. Let stand 30 minutes.
2. Meanwhile, in a small bowl, combine sugar, vinegar and salt, mixing well until sugar is dissolved. Refrigerate.
3. Drain liquid from cucumbers. Stir in vinegar mixture. Refrigerate 30 minutes or until ready to serve.

> Tip
> *   Salad can be covered and refrigerated for up to 5 days.

Spinach, Tomato and Mushroom Salad

Makes 2 Servings

Calories 258 | Carbohydrate 12 g | Fiber 4 g | Fat 21 g | Protein 7 g

8 cups spinach
1 cup cherry tomatoes,
   halved
8 oz cremini
   mushrooms, sliced
1/4 small red onion,
   sliced
3 tbsp virgin olive oil
1 tbsp lemon juice
Kosher salt
Freshly ground black
   pepper

1. Arrange spinach in 2 salad bowls. Top each with 1/2 of the tomatoes, mushrooms and onions.
2. In a small jar with a cover, add oil and lemon juice. Season with salt and pepper. Cover jar and shake vigorously to combine. Drizzle vinaigrette over salads.

Moroccan Carrot Salad

In this Moroccan-inspired salad, shredded carrots are kicked-up a notch with a spicy lemon dressing, raisings and crumbled feta cheese. Very easy to make and delightful to eat.

Makes 4 Servings

Calories 262 | Carbohydrate 17 g | Fiber 1 g | Fat 21 g | Protein 5 g

2 tsp dry harissa
2 tbsp lemon juice
5 tsp extra-virgin olive oil
Kosher salt
Freshly ground black pepper
3⁄4 lb carrots, julienned or coarsely shredded (about 2-1/2 cups)
1⁄2 cup raisins
3⁄4 cup loosely packed parsley leaves
1/3 cup crumbled feta

1. In a large bowl, whisk the harissa with the lemon juice. Gradually whisk in the oil. Season with salt and pepper.
2. Add the carrots and raisins to the dressing, tossing well to coat in the dressing.
3. Gently toss in the parsley and feta. Refrigerate until ready to serve or serve immediately.

> Tip
> * The salad can be made through step 2, covered and refrigerated for up to 6 hours. Complete step 3 before serving.

Watermelon Feta and Mint Salad

Who doesn't like the cooling, sweet, fresh taste of watermelon? Feta cheese and mint add an interesting mix of sweet and savory to this salad. It is so versatile it can be served as a side dish, small main course, or dessert. For lunch, make the full recipe for one person.

Makes 2 Servings

Calories 96 | Carbohydrate 12 g | Fiber 1 g | Fat 4 g | Protein 4 g

2 cups watermelon balls
1/4 cup crumbled feta cheese
2 tbsp fresh mint leaves

1. In a shallow bowl, gently toss watermelon balls with chopped mint and crumbled feta.

Sugar Snap Pea and Radish Salad

Fresh sugar snap peas are just delightful with their crisp and sweet taste. Their already stunning flavor is enhanced with sumac, radishes, feta cheese and a refreshing vinaigrette.

Makes 4 Servings

Calories 120 | Carbohydrate 9 g | Fiber 2 g | Fat 8 g | Protein 4 g

3/4 lb sugar snap peas trimmed, stringed, cut in half diagonally

Kosher salt

5 tsp extra-virgin olive oil

2 tsp fresh lemon juice (approx.)

1/2 tsp white wine vinegar

1/2 tsp ground sumac, divided

3 oz radishes, trimmed and thinly sliced

1/4 cup crumbled feta cheese (about 2 oz)

Freshly ground black pepper

1 tbsp coarsely chopped fresh mint

> **Tip**
> To make ahead of time, cover and refrigerate dressing and salad separately up to 24 hours.

1. Fill a large bowl with ice water; set aside.
2. In a stock pot over medium-high heat, add 6 cups water and 1 tsp salt; heat until boiling. Add peas and cook, 2 minutes or until crisp-tender. Drain and immediately transfer to bowl with ice water. Let cool, refreshing cold water as needed. Transfer to a clean kitchen towel and pat dry.
3. In a small bowl, whisk oil 1-1/2 tsp lemon juice, vinegar and 1/4 tsp sumac in a small bowl.
4. In a large bowl, combine peas, radishes and cheese. Add dressing and toss to coat. Season with salt, pepper and remaining sumac Drizzle with remaining lemon juice, if desired.
5. Serve garnished with mint.

Roasted Apple, Fennel and Pear Salad

You will drool over this delightful combination of fruit and fennel in a balsamic maple vinaigrette, topped with goat cheese and toasted walnuts.

Makes 4 Servings

Calories 261 | Carbohydrate 19 g | Fiber 5 g | Fat 19 g | Protein 7 g

½ lb red apples, cored and cut into 3/4-inch wedges

½ lb. firm pears cored and cut into 3/4-inch wedges

1 fennel bulb, cored and cut into 1/2-inch wedges

1/4 cup grapeseed oil, divided

Kosher salt

⅓ cup thinly sliced shallots

1 tsp grated ginger

2 tbsp white balsamic vinegar

1 tbsp pure maple syrup

1 lime, zest and juice

2 tsp finely chopped fresh parsley

1 tsp Dijon mustard

1/2 cup crumbled fresh goat cheese

¼ cup toasted chopped walnuts

Freshly ground black pepper

1. Preheat oven to 450°F with racks in the upper and lower third of the oven.
2. In a large bowl, combine the apples and pears with 1 tbsp of oil and 1/2 tsp salt. Transfer to a large rimmed heavy-duty baking sheet lined with foil. Spread fruit into a single layer.
3. In the same large bowl, combine the fennel, 1 tbsp of oil and 1/2 tsp salt. Transfer to a another large rimmed heavy-duty baking sheet lined with foil. Spread into a single layer.
4. Roast, turning halfway through cooking and rotating the baking sheets, 20 to 25 minutes or until browned and fork-tender. Let stand 15 minutes to cool. Transfer to a large bowl.
5. Meanwhile, in a skillet over medium heat, add the remaining oil and heat until shimmering. Add the shallots and cook, stirring often, 3 minutes or until softened and lightly browned. Add the ginger and cook, stirring, 30 seconds of until fragrant. Let stand 5 minutes to cool.
6. In a small bowl, whisk the vinegar, maple syrup, lime zest and juice, parsley, mustard, 1/4 tsp salt and 1/4 tsp pepper. Whisk the warm oil into the vinegar mixture until emulsified. Drizzle vinaigrette over the fruit mixture. Serve sprinkled with goat cheese and walnuts.

Cantaloupe and Raspberries with Tarragon and Mint

This light and refreshing side dish is like sunshine in a bowl. It makes for a colorful and welcome accompaniment or an invigorating snack.

Makes 6 Servings

Calories 217 | Carbohydrate 14 g | Fiber 4 g | Fat 19 g | Protein 1 g

1 cantaloupe, halved and seeded
Kosher salt
2 tbsp minced shallot
1 tbsp chopped fresh tarragon
1 tsp ground mustard
1/2 cup extra virgin olive oil
3 tbsp fresh lemon juice
8 oz fresh raspberries
Freshly ground black pepper
Chopped mint leaves

1. Using a melon baller, scoop balls from the cantaloupe and add to a large bowl. Season with salt.
2. In a small bowl, combine shallots, tarragon, mustard and lemon juice, Gradually whisk in oil. Season to taste with salt and pepper.
3. Drizzle vinaigrette over the cantaloupe, tossing to coat. Gently stir in raspberries. Serve garnished with mint.

Blood Orange Salad with Lemon Vinaigrette

This bright and colorful salad tastes just as good at it looks. If you want to brighten up your dinner table, this is salad is the perfect choice.

Makes 2 Servings

Calories 276 | Carbohydrate 38 g | Fiber 7 g | Fat 14 g | Protein 4 g

¼ small red onion, very thinly sliced
¼ cup rice wine vinegar
Sea salt
Freshly ground pepper
4 blood oranges
4 cups lightly packed arugula
2 tbsp extra virgin olive oil
2 tsp lemon juice
1 tbsp finely chopped mint leaves

1. In a small bowl, add the red onion and vinegar, tossing well. Season with salt and pepper. Let stand 15 minutes or until onions are softened. Drain.
2. Meanwhile, peel the oranges, removing the white pith. Using a sharp knife, thinly slice the oranges crosswise. Remove any seeds.
3. Arrange arugula on serving plates. Arrange the orange slices on the arugula. Scatter with red onions.
4. In a small jar with a cover, add the olive oil, lemon juice and mint. Cover jar and shake vigorously until combined. Drizzle vinaigrette over the salad. Season to taste with salt and pepper.

Tip
* Substitute navel oranges or tangerines for the blood oranges.

Green Beans with Tomatoes and Olives

Vegetables, herbs and citrus add wonderful contrast to crisp-tender green beans.

Makes 6 Servings

Calories 206 | Carbohydrate 16 g | Fiber 6 g | Fat 16 g | Protein 4 g

10 cherry tomatoes, halved
1/2 cup pitted kalamata olives, halved
1 shallot, minced
2 cloves garlic, minced
1/4 cup extra-virgin olive oil
1 tbsp red wine vinegar
Kosher salt
freshly ground black pepper
1-1/2 lbs green beans, trimmed and cut into 2-inch pieces
3 tbsp chopped fresh basil

1. In a medium bowl, combine tomatoes, olives, shallot, garlic, 2 tbsp oil, vinegar, 1 tsp salt and 1/4 tsp pepper. Set aside.
2. In a large skillet over medium heat, add the remaining oil and heat until shimmering. Add green beans and 1/4 tsp salt; cook, stirring often, 5 minutes or until lightly spotted. Add 1/2 cup water and cook, covered, 5 to 7 minutes or until crisp-tender.
3. Stir in tomato mixture and cook, uncovered, 2 minutes or until beans are tender and tomatoes are beginning to break down. Stir in basil and season to taste with salt and pepper. Transfer to a serving bowl.

Steamed Green Beans with Lemon-Tarragon

Makes 4 Servings

Calories 276 | Carbohydrate 38 g | Fiber 7 g | Fat 14 g | Protein 4 g

1 lb green beans, trimmed
2 tbsp finely chopped fresh tarragon
1 tbsp minced shallots
2 tbsp virgin olive oil
2 tsp lemon juice
Kosher salt
Freshly ground pepper

1. In a medium saucepan with a steamer basket, bring 1-inch water to boiling. Add green bean to the basket and steam the beans 5 minutes or until crisp-tender. Drain.
2. In a large bowl, whisk together the tarragon, shallots, oil and juice. Add green beans and toss to coat. Season to taste with salt and pepper.

Braised Green Beans with Mint and Feta

These melt-in-your-mouth green beans get a little kick from chile peppers and then are balanced with the creamy tang of feta cheese.

Makes 6 Servings

Calories 168 | Carbohydrate 17 g | Fiber 5 g | Fat 10 g | Protein 5 g

3 tbsp virgin olive oil
1 onion, finely chopped
4 cloves garlic, minced
2 tsps dried oregano
Pinch red chile flakes
1-1/2 lbs green beans, trimmed and cut 2-1/2 inch pieces
1/2 tsp baking soda
1-1/2 cups water
1 can (14.5 oz) diced tomatoes, with juice
1 tbsp tomato paste
1 tsp Kosher salt
1/4 tsp freshly ground black pepper
2 tbsp chopped fresh mint
Red wine vinegar
1/2 cup crumbled feta cheese (about 2 oz)

1. Preheat oven to 275°F with an oven rack in the lower third.
2. In a Dutch oven over medium heat, add the oil and heat until shimmering. Add onion and cook, stirring often, 3 minutes or until softened. Add garlic, oregano and chili flakes; cook, stirring, 1 minute or until fragrant.
3. Stir in water, baking soda and green beans; cook until simmering. Reduce heat to medium-low and cook, stirring occasionally, for 10 minutes. Stir in tomatoes with juice, tomato paste, salt and pepper.
4. Cover pot and bake, 45 minutes or until beans are tender and sauce is slightly thickened.
5. Add mint and stir in vinegar to taste. Serve sprinkled with feta.

> **Variation:**
> * ***Braised Green Beans with Golden Petite Potatoes:*** For a heartier side dish, add 1 lbs Yukon gold potatoes, cut into 1-inch pieces. Add with the tomatoes in step 3.

Note: This recipe utilizes a technique from Cooks Illustrated that boils the green beans in baking soda. The beans come out tender, but not mushy. Braising the beans in tomatoes, neutralizes any soda taste.

Porcini Mushroom Risotto with Peas

Risotto is one of those dishes that is loved by many, but the home cook is often afraid to tackle. Here a couple of techniques make the process and end result delicious. The addition of porcini mushroom powder and sweet peas takes it over the top.

Makes 4 Servings

Calories 221 | Carbohydrate 35 g | Fiber 2 g | Fat 5 g | Protein 7 g

2-1/2 cups reduced-sodium chicken broth
1 tbsp virgin olive oil
1/4 cup chopped shallots
1 clove garlic, minced
3/4 cup arborio rice
Kosher salt
2 tsp porcini mushroom powder
1/2 cup dry white wine
3/4 cup frozen peas, thawed
1/4 cup grated low fat parmesan cheese
Freshly ground black pepper

1. In a medium saucepan over medium heat, add broth and heat until simmering. Reduce heat to low and keep broth steaming but not simmering.
2. In a Dutch oven over medium heat add oil and heat until shimmering. Add the shallots and cook, stirring, 2 minutes or until softened. Add the garlic and cook, stirring, 1 minute or until fragrant.
3. Add rice and 1 tsp salt; cook, stirring, 3 minutes or until rice is coated and turning opaque. Stir in broth and wine; cook, stirring frequently, 25 to 30 minutes or until rice is creamy and al dente and most of the liquid is absorbed. Stir in peas during the last 5 minutes of cooking.
4. Remove from the heat and stir in cheese.
5. Season to taste with salt and pepper. Serve.

Sweet and Savory Basmati Rice Salad

Basmati rice gets a whole new depth of flavor in this salad with dates, green onions, toasted almonds, and a bright citrus vinaigrette.

Makes 8 Servings

Calories 256 | Carbohydrate 36 g | Fiber 3 g | Fat 12 g | Protein 4 g

1 cup basmati rice
Kosher salt
3/4 cup slivered
  almonds
3/4 cup chopped dates
4 green onions, thinly
  sliced
1/4 cup chopped fresh
  parsley leaves
2-1/2 tbsp lemon juice
1 tsp grated orange zest
  plus 2 tbsp juice from
  1 orange
1/2 tsp ground
  cinnamon
Freshly ground black
  pepper
1/4 cup extra virgin
  olive oil

> Tip
> * Salad can be covered
>   tightly and refrigerated up
>   to 1 day. Remove from
>   refrigerator and let stand
>   until room temperature.

1. In a medium skillet over medium-heat, add rice and cook, stirring often, 7 minutes or until fragrant and grains are just turning opaque.
2. Bring a large pot of water to a boil. Stir in 2 tsp salt and the rice; cook, uncovered, 9 to 11 minutes or until rice is tender. Drain rice, transfer rice to a baking sheet and spread out rice. Let stand, 20 minutes or until cooled completely.
3. Meanwhile in the medium skillet over medium heat, add the almonds and cook, shaking, 3 minutes or until fragrant and lightly toasted. Set aside. To cool.
4. Transfer rice to a large serving bowl. Stir in dates, onions and parsley.
5. In a medium bowl, whisk together lemon juice, 2 tbsp orange juice, 1 tsp orange zest, cinnamon and 1/4 tsp pepper. Slowly whisk in oil. Season with salt and pepper to taste. Drizzle over rice mixture and toss to combine. Let stand 20 minutes. Serve.
6. Adjust seasonings and let stand until flavors blend, about 20 minutes. Serve at room temperature.

Simple Lebanese Rice

This wonderful twist on traditional Western rice is so interesting and delicious that you will want to serve it alongside many a Mediterranean main dish.

Makes 6 Servings

- -

Calories 415 | Carbohydrate 77 g | Fiber 27 g | Fat 7 g | Protein 49 g

2 cups long grain rice, rinsed and drained
1 cup broken vermicelli pasta
2-1/2 tbsp virgin olive oil
Kosher salt
1/2 cup toasted pine nuts (optional)

Tip
* To toast pine nuts, in a medium small skillet over medium heat, add the nut and sauté, swirling nuts in pan, 1 to 2 minutes or until light golden brown. Transfer nuts to a plate and let cool. You can use the same saucepan you are going to use in step 2. You do not need to clean the pan before cooking your rice.

1. In a medium bowl, add the rice and cover with water. Let stand 15 minutes; drain.
2. In a medium, heavy-bottom saucepan over medium-high heat, add the oil and heat until shimmering. Add the vermicelli and cook, stirring, 2 minutes or until golden brown. Add the rice, stirring, 2 minutes or until rice is coated in oil. Season with salt. Stir in 3-1/2 cups water. Bring to a boil.
3. Reduce heat to low, cover and cook, 15 minutes or until rice is al dente and water is absorbed. Remove from heat, cover and let stand 5 minutes.
4. Remove cover and fluff rice with a fork. Spoon rice into a serving bowl. Serve garnished with toasted pine nuts, if using.

Note: If using pine nuts, the nutritional values are:
Cal 469 | Carbs 78 g | Fiber 2 g | Fat 12 g | Protein 10 g

Tabbouleh

This traditional Lebanese salad is a cornucopia of fresh vegetables and herbs with a delectable lemon-herb dressing.

Makes 4 Servings

Calories 202 | Carbohydrate 18 g | Fiber 8 g | Fat 15 g | Protein 5g

1/4 cup fine bulgur wheat

1/2 lb tomatoes, finely chopped

1 bunch green onions, thinly sliced

3 cups chopped fresh flat-leaf parsley (about 3 large bunches)

1/4 cup chopped fresh mint

1 clove garlic, minced

2 lemons, juice of Kosher salt

3 tbsp extra virgin olive oil

1 large head romaine lettuce, coarsely chopped

Tips
* Substitute 6 cups coarsely chopped kale for the romaine.

1. In a medium bowl, add the bulgur and cover with water by 1/2-inch. Let stand 20 minutes or until slightly softened. Using a fine mesh strainer lined with cheesecloth, drain bulgur, pressing down to squeeze out water.
2. Transfer bulgur to a large bowl. Add the tomatoes, onions, parsley, mint, garlic and juice tossing to combine. Season to taste with salt. Cover and refrigerate for 2 to 3 hours or until the bulgur absorbs more liquids and swells.
3. Drizzle in the olive oil, tossing well. Season to taste with salt. Add the lettuce, tossing to coat. Let stand 15 minutes. Serve.

Variation
* To serve as an appetizer for 6, omit the romaine and spoon tabbouleh on endive leaves.

Cauliflower Couscous

In this classic Israeli-style couscous, the addition of cauliflower florets and chopped dates, makes it extra special.

Makes 4 Servings

Calories 398 | Carbohydrate 66 g | Fiber 6 g | Fat 11 g | Protein 11 g

1-1/2 cups Israeli
   couscous
3 tbsp virgin olive oil
3 cups cauliflower
   florets
1 shallot, sliced
Kosher salt
Freshly ground black
   pepper.
1/4 cup chopped dates
Pinch cinnamon
1/2 cup firmly packed
   chopped parsley
1 tbsp red wine vinegar

1. Cook couscous according to the package directions. Drain and rinse with cold water. Transfer to a large bowl and toss with 1 tbsp olive oil

2. In a large skillet, add remaining oil and heat until shimmering. Add cauliflower and shallots; cook, stirring often, 6 minutes. Season with salt and pepper. Stir in dates and cinnamon and cook, stirring often, 2 minutes or until cauliflower is crisp tender and flavors are melded.

3. Stir cauliflower mixture, parsley and vinegar into couscous.

4. Season to taste with salt and pepper. Serve.

Lebanese Potatoes

These lovely potatoes, known as Batata Harra, are crispy and served in a delicious sauce of garlic, cilantro, paprika, and cayenne pepper. They are then finished with parsley and lemon juice for an out-of-this-world taste.

Makes 4 Servings

Calories 237 | Carbohydrate 33 g | Fiber 4 g | Fat 11 g | Protein 4 g

1-1/2 lbs red potatoes, scrubbed and cut into 1-1/2-inch chunks
3 tbsp olive oil
2 tbsp minced garlic
1/2 cup minced cilantro
1-3/4 tbsp paprika
1 tsp cayenne
Kosher salt
2 tbsp minced parsley
2 tbsp fresh lemon juice

1. Rinse potatoes in cold water until water runs clear. Bring a pot of salted water to a boil. Add potatoes and boil 5 minutes or until they begin to soften and become slightly translucent. Drain and let completely air dry on paper towels.
2. In a saucepan over medium-low heat, add 2 tbsp oil and garlic; cook, covered, 3 minutes or until softened and pale gold. Add the cilantro and cook, stirring, 1 to 2 minutes or until wilted. Transfer sauce to a large bowl and set aside.
3. In a large skillet over medium heat, add remaining oil and heat until shimmering. Add the potatoes and cook, flipping occasionally (do not stir), 5 to 7 minutes or until browned and crispy on all sides.
4. Transfer potatoes to the bowl of sauce. Sprinkle with paprika and cayenne. Season with salt and toss gently. Transfer mixture to a serving bowl. Garnish with parsley. Serve drizzled with lemon juice. Serve warm.

Roasted Vegetables with Garlic and Thyme

This colorful side dish abounds with a nutritious and mouthwatering combination of beets, carrots, and Brussels sprouts. Roasting with garlic and thyme builds that flavor of this wonderful addition to any meal.

Makes 8 Servings

Calories 146 | Carbohydrate 22 g | Fiber 7 g | Fat 6 g | Protein 5 g

3 tbsp olive oil
4 medium red beets
  (about 1-1/2 lbs total)
1-1/2 lbs carrots, peeled
  and cut into 1-inch
  thick rounds
1-1/2 lbs Brussels
  sprouts, trimmed and
  halved lengthwise
8 large cloves garlic,
  unpeeled
1 tbsp chopped fresh
  thyme
Kosher salt
Freshly ground black
  pepper

Tips
* When working with beets, wear kitchen gloves to prevent your hands from discoloring.

1. Preheat oven to 375°F.
2. Cut greens from beets, leaving 1-inch stem on. (Greens can be discarded or saved for another use.) Do not cut root end. Scrub beets well.
3. Brush beets all over with 1 tbsp oil. Arrange the beets in a 9-inch square glass baking dish and cover with foil. Roast 30 minutes.
4. Meanwhile, arrange the carrots, Brussels sprouts and garlic in a large glass baking dish. Toss with the remaining oil, 3/4 tsp salt and 1/4 tsp pepper.
5. Keep the beets in the oven. Add the carrot mixture to oven and roast, stirring occasionally, 60 minutes or until vegetables are fork tender.
6. Transfer the beets to a cutting board. Let cool.
7. Stir the thyme into the carrot mixture and continue roasting for another 10 minutes.
8. When the beets are cool enough to handle, peel and cut them into 1-inch chunks. Transfer beets to a serving bowl.
9. Add the carrot mixture to the beets, tossing well. Season to taste with salt and pepper. Serve.

MEATLESS MAINS

Turkish Stuffed Eggplant

This beloved eggplant dish, known as Imam Bayildi, has as many variations. This version is a traditional, mouth-watering main course. You may be surprised that eggplant is a fruit, so along with the tomatoes, you have a wonderful serving of fruit!

Makes 4 Servings

Calories 404 | Carbohydrate 41 g | Fiber 18 g | Fat 24 g | Protein 11 g

4 small eggplants,
  halved lengthwise
1/4 cup olive oil
1 medium onion, minced
4 cloves garlic, minced
1-1/2 lbs plum tomatoes,
  peeled and chopped
2 tsp sugar
Kosher salt
2 tsps minced fresh
  oregano leaves
1/4 tsp ground
  cinnamon
1/8 tsp cayenne pepper
2 ozs Pecorino Romano,
  grated (about 1 cup)
1/4 cup pine nuts,
  toasted
1 tbsp red wine vinegar
1/4 cup finely chopped
  fresh parsley leaves
2 tbsp finely chopped
  fresh dill
¼ cup water
2 tbsp lemon juice

Tip
* Cook the eggplant through step 2 and set aside. Follow steps 3 and 4 and set aside. Eggplant and filling can be stored several hours before completing steps 5 to 7.

1. Preheat oven to 450°F.
2. Line a rimmed baking sheet with foil and brush with olive oil. Arrange eggplants on baking sheet and bake 20 minutes, or until the skin begins to shrivel. Transfer, cut-side down, to a colander set over a sink. Let stand 30 minutes to drain.
3. Meanwhile, in a large skillet over medium heat add the oil and heat until shimmering. Add the onions and cook, stirring often, 5 minutes or until the onions are softened. Add the garlic and cook, stirring, 1 minute or until fragrant. Transfer mixture to a large bowl.
4. Stir in the tomatoes, parsley, dill, 1 tsp sugar and 1 tbsp oil. Season with salt.
5. Transfer the eggplants, cut side up to the skillet. Season with salt. Spoon onion tomato mixture into each eggplant.
6. In a medium bowl, combine the remaining oil, the remaining sugar, the water and lemon juice. Drizzle mixture all over the eggplants.
7. Cover the skillet and cook over low heat 1 to 1-1/2 hours, basting occasionally with the pan juices and adding more water if needed, until the eggplants are almost flat and the juices are caramelized. Remove from heat, spoon juices over eggplant and let cool in the skillet. Serve at room temperature.

Moroccan Root Vegetable Tagine

Ras el hanout, a North African spice blend marries the flavors of this cornucopia of fall harvest vegetables and tomatoes for a highly satisfying dish. When topped with a dollop of lemon yogurt, the cooling sensation balances the spiciness of the vegetables.

Makes 4 Servings

Calories 212 | Carbohydrate 38 g | Fiber 7 g | Fat 4 g | Protein 7 g

1 tbsp virgin olive oil
1 red onion, chopped
1 tbsp ras el hanout
1 can (28 oz) whole peeled tomatoes
1 lb sweet potatoes, chopped
1 lb parsnips, chopped
1/2 lb turnips, chopped
1/3 cup golden raisins
Kosher salt
freshly ground black pepper
1/2 cup fat free plain Greek yogurt
1 tsp fresh lemon juice
1 cup loosely packed parsley leaves, chopped

Tip
* You can use 2 large peeled tomatoes in place of the canned.

1. In a Dutch oven or large heavy-bottom stockpot over medium heat, add the oil and heat until shimmering. Add the onion and ras el hanout; cook, stirring often, 3 minutes or until the onion is softened.
2. Gently crush the tomatoes with your hands and add to the pot with the onions. Add the sweet potatoes, parsnips, turnips, raisins and 1-1/2 cups water. Season with salt and pepper; cook, until boiling. Reduce heat to medium and simmer, stirring occasionally, 20 minutes or until the vegetables are tender.
3. Meanwhile, in a medium bowl, combine the yogurt and lemon juice. Season to taste with salt and pepper. Set aside.
4. Transfer vegetable tagine into a serving dish. Garnish with parsley. Serve with yogurt mixture on the side.

Delightful Greek Hand Pies

These mouthwatering hand pies have many things going for them including, wonderful greens, savory feta, and seasoning all wrapped in a half-moon dough.

Makes 4 Servings

Calories 609 | Carbohydrate 77 g | Fiber 11 g | Fat 27 g | Protein 19 g

1 lb fresh pizza dough
2 tbsp virgin olive oil
6 green onions, white and light green parts sliced
1-1/2 lbs mixed greens, such as spinach and arugula, coarsely chopped
1/2 cup chopped dill
1/2 cup chopped fresh oregano
1/2 cup crumbled feta cheese (about 2 oz)
2 tbsp freshly grated Parmigiano-Reggiano cheese
1 large egg
Kosher salt
Freshly ground black pepper
All-purpose flour

1. In a large skillet over medium heat, add the oil and heat until shimmering. Add the green onions and cook , stirring often, 3 minutes or until softened. Add the greens and cook, stirring, 2 minutes or until wilted. Stir in the dill and oregano; cook, stirring, 1 minute. Transfer mixture to a colander and let cool. Squeeze out any excess liquid.
2. In a large bowl, lightly beat the egg. Stir in the greens, feta, Parmigiano-Reggiano, 1/2 tsp salt and 1/4 tsp pepper.
3. Preheat oven to 400°F.
4. Lightly flour a large, rimmed baking sheet. Set aside.
5. Divide the dough into 4 equal pieces. Lightly flour a work surface and roll out each piece into an 8-inch diameter circle.
6. Mound one-fourth of the filling on the lower half of each circle. Fold the dough over to make a half-moon; press the edge of the dough to seal. Using a lightly floured fork, crimp the edges of the dough.
7. Transfer the hand pies to the prepared baking sheet.
8. Bake 1 hour or until the crust is golden brown and the filling is hot. Serve immediately.

Quinoa Edamame Toss

What do you get when you combine quinoa, edamame and fresh arugula? A power house of nutrients with an extraordinary taste!

Makes 2 Servings

Calories 472 | Carbohydrate 51 g | Fiber 12 g | Fat 25 g | Protein 20 g

1/2 cup uncooked quinoa, rinsed and drained
1 cup water
1 cup frozen shelled edamame, thawed
2 medium tomatoes, seeded and chopped
1/2 cup chopped red onion
1 cup fresh arugula
2 tbsp virgin olive oil
1 lemon
Kosher salt
Freshly ground black pepper
1/4 cup crumbled feta cheese (about 2 oz)
2 tbsp fresh basil, chopped

1. In a medium saucepan over medium-high heat, combine quinoa and water; heat until boiling. Reduce heat to medium-low, cover and cook, 10 minutes. Stir in edamame. Cover and cook 5 more minutes or until quinoa is tender and liquid is absorbed.
2. In a large bowl, combine quinoa mixture, tomatoes, onions and arugula.
3. In a small bowl, grate 1 tsp lemon zest. Squeeze 2 tbsp lemon juice into the bowl. Whisk in olive oil, 1/2 tsp salt and 1/4 tsp pepper. Stir in 2 tbsp cheese and the basil. Pour over quinoa mixture, tossing to coat.
4. Sprinkle with remaining chese. Serve at room temperature.

Navy Bean and Fennel Salad

Meaty navy beans converge with crispy sliced fennel and a creamy lemon garlic dressing for a scrumptious main salad.

Makes 2 Servings

Calories 318 | Carbohydrate 47 g | Fiber 16 g | Fat 8 g | Protein 19 g

1 lemon
1 clove garlic, minced
3 tbsp Greek yogurt
   (approx.)
1 fennel bulb, stems and
   roots removed
1 green onion, sliced
2 tbsp finely chopped
   fresh parsley leaves
1 cup water
1 can (15.5 oz) navy
   beans, rinsed and
   drained
Kosher salt
Freshly ground black
   pepper
1/4 cup shaved
   parmesan cheese

1. In a small bowl, grate the zest of the lemon and 1 tbsp freshly squeezed lemon juice from the lemon. Stir in the garlic and 2 tbsp yogurt. Set aside.
2. Slice the fennel bulb in half and remove the core. Using a mandoline, thinly slice the remaining bulb. Transfer to a large bowl.
3. Stir in the green onion, parsley, and the lemon garlic mixture, adding more yogurt as necessary. Season to taste with salt and pepper.
4. Serve garnished with shaved cheese.

Tip
*   Salad can be covered and refrigerated for up to 24 hours.

Chickpea, Zucchini and Tomatoes with Pesto

A delicious meal using nutritious healthy vegetables and power-packed chickpeas which are combined and then finished with a spinach pesto.

Makes 4 Servings

Calories 439 | Carbohydrate 28 g | Fiber 10 g | Fat 34 g | Protein 13 g

1 large zucchini, sliced
Kosher salt
Freshly ground black
 pepper
3/4 cup walnuts,
 toasted
1-1/2 cups lightly packed
 spinach
1/2 cup fresh basil
 leaves
2 garlic cloves, peeled
1 lemon
1/3 cup virgin olive oil
1 can chickpeas, drained
 and rinsed
2 cups cherry tomatoes,
 halved

1. Preheat oven to 425°F.
2.. On a foil-lined backing sheet sprayed with nonstick cooking spray, arrange zucchini and season with salt and pepper. Roast 25 minutes, or until lightly browned and tender.
3. Meanwhile, add walnuts to a food processor or blend and pulse until walnuts are a fine meal. Do not over process.
4. Add the spinach, basil, garlic, juice and zest from lemon, 2-1/2 tbsp oil, 1/4 tsp salt and 1/4 tsp pepper, pulsing until the mixture is combined, scraping down the sides of the container as needed. Slowly blend in the remaining olive oil.
5. In a large bowl, add the zucchini, chickpeas and cherry tomatoes. Drizzle with pesto sauce, gently tossing to combine. Serve immediately or cover and refrigerate up to 3 days.

Tip
* To toast walnuts, heat a
 small skillet over medium-
 high heat. Add walnuts,
 tossing often, 2 minutes or
 until walnuts are fragrant.
 Let cool.

Chickpea and Chopped Vegetable Salad

This exceptional combination of healthy and tasty chickpeas, chopped vegetables, herbs, and cheese is a satisfying main course salad or a hearty side salad.

Makes 8 Servings

Calories 436 | Carbohydrate 43 g | Fiber 13 g | Fat 23 g | Protein 17 g

1 medium cucumber, peeled
1 pint cherry tomatoes
Kosher salt
3 tbsp red wine vinegar
2 tbsp finely chopped mint leaves
1 clove garlic, minced
3 tbsp extra virgin olive oil
1 small yellow bell pepper, stemmed, seeded and chopped
1/2 cup chopped pitted kalamata olives
1/2 small red onion, minced
1 can (28 oz) chickpeas, drained and rinsed
1/4 cup lightly packed chopped parsley leaves
1 cup crumbled feta cheese (about 4 oz)
Freshly ground black pepper

1. Peel cucumbers and cut in half lengthwise. Remove seeds and cut into about 1/2-inch pieces. Transfer to a colander. Cut tomatoes into quarters and add to cucumbers. Sprinkle with 1 tsp salt, tossing to combine and let drain about 15 to 30 minutes.
2. In a small bowl, whisk vinegar, mint leaves and garlic. Slowly whisk in oil.
3. In a large bowl, add bell pepper, olives, red onions, chickpeas, parsley and the cucumber tomato mixture.Pour vinaigrette over the top and toss gently to combine. Let stand 10 minutes.
4. Toss in feta cheese. Season to taste with salt and pepper. Serve.

Brussels Sprouts and Chickpea Salad

An easy and simple way to give a distinctive flavor to a chickpea salad with the additional of roasted Brussels sprouts. Great as a hearty main dish or as a side dish to serve alongside grilled chicken, pork, or fish.

Makes 3 Servings

Calories 455 | Carbohydrate 42 g | Fiber 15 g | Fat 27 g | Protein 19 g

1/4 cup thinly sliced red onion

12 oz Brussels sprouts, cleaned and halved

1 can (15.5 oz) chickpeas, drained and rinsed

3 tbsp virgin olive oil, divided

1 lemon

Freshly ground black pepper

1/2 cup sun dried tomatoes, thinly sliced

2 tbsp chopped parsley leaves

1 cup crumbled feta cheese (about 4 oz)

Kosher salt

Tip
* This recipe makes 3 servings as a main dish or 5 to 6 servings as a side dish.

1. Preheat oven to 400°F.
2. In a small bowl of cold water, soak onion for 10 minutes. Drain and set aside.
3. Grate 2 tsp of the lemon zest and set aside. Squeeze 1-1/2 tbsp juice from the lemon and set aside.
4. In a large bowl, add the Brussels sprouts, chickpeas, 2 tbsp oil, the lemon zest and 1/2 tsp pepper, stirring well. On a foil-lined baking sheet, spread the Brussels sprout mixture and roast, tossing once, 15 minutes or until the Brussels sprouts are nicely browned and crisp-tender. Let cool.
5. In a large serving bowl, add the tomatoes, parsley, feta cheese, the Brussels sprout and chickpea mixture. Drizzle with the remaining oil and lemon juice, tossing well to coat. Season to taste with salt and pepper. Serve warm.

Antipasto and Amaranth Salad

Serve this mouth-watering antipasto combination with nutrient-dense amaranth. With it's tasty combination of artichokes, peppers and herbs, this dish is sure to become one of your favorites.

Makes 6 Servings

Calories 474 | Carbohydrate 44 g | Fiber 6 g | Fat 25 g | Protein 20 g

3 cups water
1 cup amaranth
1 can (8 oz) artichoke hearts, drained and quartered
1-1/2 cups pepperoncini, drained and sliced into rings
1 red bell pepper, stemmed, seeded and chopped
8 baby bella mushrooms, sliced
6 oz Provolone cheese, cut into 1/4 inch cubes
1/2 cup coarsely chopped Kalamata olives
3 tbsp chopped fresh parsley leaves
1/2 cup Italian salad dressing

1. In medium saucepan over medium-high heat, heat water until boiling. Stir in amaranth, cover, and reduce heat to medium-low; simmer 20 minutes or until water is absorbed. Let stand until cool.
2. Meanwhile, in a large bowl, combine artichokes, pepperoncini, bell pepper, mushrooms, cheese, olives and parsley.
3. Stir in barley. Drizzle 1/3 cup salad dressing over salad mixture. Cover and refrigerate for 2 hours.
4. Toss salad mixture. Add more dressing to taste. Season to taste with salt and pepper.

Variation:
* Add 1/2 lb Italian salami, cut into 1/4 inch cubes in step 2.

Garlic and Herb Lentil Salad

Garlic lovers are going to find bliss with this green lentil salad and its infusion of herbs and spices.

Makes 3 Servings

Calories 417 | Carbohydrate 49 g | Fiber 9 g | Fat 19 g | Protein 17 g

1 cup green lentils, rinsed and picked over
3 cups water
1/4 cup virgin olive oil, divided
7 cloves garlic, minced
2 lemons
1-1/2 tsp ground cumin
1/4 tsp ground allspice
3/4 cup lightly packed fresh parsley leaves, finely chopped
1/2 cup lightly packed fresh mint leaves, finely chopped
Kosher salt
Freshly ground black pepper

Tip
* Salad can be covered and refrigerated up to 2 days. Let stand until room temperature before serving.

1. In a medium saucepan over medium-high heat, add the lentils and water; heat until boiling, then reduce heat and simmer 20 to 25 minutes or until lentils are tender. Drain. Transfer to a medium bowl.
2. Meanwhile, In a medium skillet over medium heat, add 2 tbsp oil and heat until shimmering. Add garlic and cook, stirring, 2 minutes or until garlic is fragrant.
3. Squeeze 1/4 cup lemon juice into a bowl. Whisk in remaining oil, cumin and allspice. Pour into skillet with garlic. Cook over medium heat, stirring, about 1 minute or until heated through. Pour over lentils.
4. Stir in parsley and mint. Season to taste with salt and pepper. Serve warm or at room temperature.

Freekeh with Chickpeas, Carrots and Raisins

Power grain freekeh, with its nutty taste is partnered with chickpeas and carrots. A spicy North African seasoning, cooling yogurt, and sweet raisins round out the myriad of flavors in this unique and inviting dish.

Makes 4 Servings

Calories 432 | Carbohydrate 67 g | Fiber 14 g | Fat 14 g | Protein 14 g

1/2 cup freekeh, rinsed
Kosher salt
2 medium carrots, cut lengthwise and then cut crosswise into 2-inch pieces
1 onion, coarsely chopped
6 tsp virgin olive oil, divided
2 tsp ras el hanout
1 cup cooked chickpeas
1 cup diced tomatoes
3/4 cup raisins
1/2 cup fat free Greek yogurt
1/4 cup roasted almonds, coarsely chopped
Fresh cilantro leaves

1. In a small saucepan over medium-high heat, add the freekeh, 1-1/2 cups water and a pinch of salt; heat until boiling. Reduce heat and cook, stirring often, 15 minutes or until freekeh is tender and water is absorbed. Set aside.

2. In a large skillet over medium-heat, add 1 tbsp oil and heat until shimmering. Add the carrots and onions and cook until the carrot and onions soften and the onion starts to turn brown. Stir in the ras el hanout and cook, stirring, 30 second or until fragrant. Add the chickpeas, tomatoes, raisins and 1/2 cup water. Season with salt and pepper. Heat until boiling. Reduce heat and simmer, covered, 6 minutes or until the carrots are tender.

3. In a small bowl, combine the yogurt and the remaining oil. Season to taste with salt and pepper.

4. Transfer freekeh into individual serving bowls. Ladle the carrot and onion mixture over the freekeh. Add a dollop of the yogurt to each. Serve.

Quinoa, Collard Greens, Pomegranate Seeds and Pine Nut Salad

If you're surprised to see a southern United States staple like collard greens in a Mediterranean cookbook, don't be. These wonderful greens hold up well with grain salads and are the new darling of nutrient-rich cuisine.

Makes 4 Servings

Calories 490 | Carbohydrate 44 g | Fiber 10 g | Fat 32 g | Protein 12 g

6 tbsp virgin olive oil
2 small garlic cloves crushed
1 cup quinoa, rinsed and patted dry
2 cups water
Kosher salt
1/4 cup fresh lemon juice (about 2 lemons)
1 lb collard greens, thinly sliced
1 cup coarsely chopped parsley
2 tbsp green onions, thinly sliced
3/4 cup pomegranate seeds
1/3 cup pine nuts
Freshly ground black pepper

1. In a medium saucepan over medium-high heat, add 1 tbsp oil and heat until shimmering. Add the garlic and cook, stirring, about 2 minutes or until lightly browned. Add the quinoa and cook, stirring, about 2 minutes or until the quinoa is lightly toasted. Stir in 2 cups water and 1 tsp salt; heat until boiling. Reduce heat, cover, and cook 15 minutes or until water is absorbed. Let cool.

2. Remove the garlic cloves and transfer to a large bowl. Mash the garlic and 1/2 tsp salt into a paste. Whisk in the lemon juice and the remaining olive oil.

3. Stir the quinoa into the large bowl. Add the collard greens, parsley, onions, pomegranate seeds and pine nuts. Season with salt and pepper.

4. Serve at room temperature.

FISH AND SEAFOOD

Herb Roasted Sea Bass

Sea Bass, a meaty saltwater fish, is roasted in complementary herbs with lemons and garlic to make a deliciously fresh main dish.

Makes 2 Servings

Calories 255 | Carbohydrate 7 g | Fiber 3 g | Fat 14 g | Protein 27 g

1 lemon, halved
5 tsp extra virgin olive oil
2 tsp lemon juice
1/2 tsp dried oregano
2 cloves garlic
Kosher salt
Freshly ground black pepper
2 5-oz skinless sea bass fillets (about 3/4 inch thick)

1. Preheat oven to 475°F.
2. In a small bowl, squeeze 2 tsp lemon juice from one half. Set aside remaining half. Whisk in 3 tsp oil and oregano. Season with salt and pepper. Set aside.
3. Brush an 11 by 7-inch glass baking dish with the remaining oil.
4. Arrange fish in prepared dish, turning to coat in oil. Season fish with salt and pepper. Place garlic around fish. Spoon 1/2 tbsp lemon mixture over fish.
5. Bake fish, 12 minutes or until fish is opaque and flakes easily when tested with a fork. Let fish stand 5 minutes.
6. Meanwhile, cut remaining lemon half into wedges. Transfer fish to serving plates and top with remaining sauce. Arrange lemon wedges around fish. Serve immediately.

Baked Snapper with Tomatoes and Olives

Turn your snapper fillets into a firm but flaky Mediterranean entrée bursting with flavor created by fresh tomatoes, olives, and a careful blend of herbs and spices.

Makes 4 Servings

Calories 280 | Carbohydrate 6 g | Fiber 2 g | Fat 14 g | Protein 30 g

3 tbsp virgin olive oil

4 5 oz pieces snapper fillet

Fine sea salt

Freshly ground black pepper

1/2 tsp ground fennel

1/2 cup pitted Niçoise olives

2 tbsp dry white wine

1 lb tomatoes, seeded and cut into one-inch pieces

1/4 cup lightly packed torn fresh basil leaves

1. Preheat oven to 400°F.
2. In 13- by 9-inch glass baking dish add the oil. Heat oil in the oven until shimmering.
3. Cut a few shallow slits into the skin of each fillet.
4. Season fillets with salt, pepper and fennel.
5. Place the fish in the baking dish skin-side down to coat in the oil and immediately flip over to skin-side up. Scatter olives around the fish. Drizzle with wine.
6. Bake for 6 to 8 minutes or until the fish is opaque and flakes easily when tested with a fork.
7. Season tomatoes with salt and pepper. Scatter tomatoes around fish, about 2 minutes before the end of the roasting time.
8. Serve fish immediately with olives and tomatoes scattered around the fish.

Bass with Sweet and Sour Agrodolce Sauce

A simple way to prepare delicious striped bass with Mediterranean style vegetables, fresh herbs, and agrodolce sauce.

Makes 4 Servings

Calories 433 | Carbohydrate 21 g | Fiber 5 g | Fat 24 g | Protein 31 g

1/3 cup-virgin olive oil
3 large shallots, finely chopped
6 medium cloves garlic, coarsely chopped
4 sprigs fresh thyme
1/8 tsp red pepper flakes
1/4 cup red wine
1 tbsp lightly packed brown sugar
1-1/2 tbsp balsamic vinegar
4 5 oz striped bass fillets, pin bones removed
Kosher salt
Freshly ground black pepper
12 oz mixed mushrooms (shiitake, chanterelle and/or oyster), cut into pieces if large
2 cups cherry tomatoes

1. Preheat the oven to 375°F.
2. In a small saucepan over low heat, add 3 tbsp oil, shallots, garlic, thyme and pepper flakes. Cook, stirring often, 8 minutes or until the shallots are softened and the garlic is fragrant. Discard thyme sprigs. Transfer 1 tbsp of the oil to a large skillet and set aside.
3. Add wine to the saucepan and cook, scraping up any browned bits from the bottom of the pan, 5 minutes or until the wine is reduced by half. Stir in sugar and vinegar. Cook over medium-low heat, stirring occasionally, about 5 minutes or until the sauce is thickened and caramelized.
4. Add the remaining olive oil to the skillet cook over medium-high heat until shimmering. Season fillets with salt and pepper. Add the fillets, skin-side down, and cook 5 minutes. Flip fillets over and cook, 3 minutes or until fish is opaque and flakes easily when tested with a fork.
5. Transfer fish to serving plates. Serve drizzle with warm agrodolce sauce.

Lemon Salmon with Lima Beans

Lima beans are the perfect vegetable to serve with salmon fillets to bring out the true Mediterranean delicacy and flavor of salmon.

Makes 4 Servings

Calories 324 | Carbohydrate 21 g | Fiber 5 g | Fat 12 g | Protein 35 g

1 lemon, halved
1/4 cup plain Greek
   yogurt
1/2 tsp paprika
2 tsp virgin olive oil
2 cloves garlic, thinly
   sliced
1/2 tsp dried oregano
Pinch red pepper flakes
8 oz frozen baby lima
   beans
Kosher salt
Freshly ground black
   pepper
1 tbsp chopped fresh
   parsley
4 5-oz center cut
   salmon fillets

1. Grate the zest from 1/2 of the lemon and set aside. In a small bowl, squeeze 2 tsp lemon juice. Stir in yogurt and 1/4 tsp paprika.
2. Preheat the broiler.
3. In a medium saucepan over medium heat, add 1 tsp oil and heat until shimmering. Add the garlic, oregano and pepper flakes; cook, stirring, about 1 to 2 minutes or until the garlic is golden brown.
4. Add the lima beans, 3/4 cup water and the lemon zest; cook, stirring often, until simmering. Reduce heat to medium-low, partially cover the saucepan and cook, about 20 minutes or until the beans are tender. Drain beans and return to saucepan. Season with salt and pepper. Stir in the parsley, 1 tbsp of the yogurt mixture and the remaining oil.
5. Meanwhile, place salmon on a baking sheet lined with foil. Season with salt and remaining paprika. Slice 2 thin slices from remaining lemon half. Arrange a slice on top of each piece of salmon. Broil 6 to 8 minutes or until salmon flakes easily when tested with a fork.
6. Transfer salmon to individual serving plates. Top with remaining yogurt mixture. Spoon lima beans around salmon. Serve immediately.

Lemon-Herb Salmon with Sicilian Caponata

Bring the flavors of Sicily home with this lemon and herb seasoned salmon paired with a delightful vegetable caponata.

Makes 4 Servings

Calories 373 | Carbohydrate 20 g | Fiber 7 g | Fat 20 g | Protein 31 g

1 medium eggplant, cut into 1-inch pieces
1 red bell pepper, cut into 1-inch pieces
1 summer squash, cut into 1-inch pieces
1 small onion, cut into 1-inch pieces
1-1/2 cups cherry tomatoes
3 tbsp virgin olive oil
1 tsp Kosher salt, divided
1/2 tsp ground black pepper, divided
2 tbsp capers, rinsed and chopped
1 tbsp red-wine vinegar
2 tsp honey
4 5-oz salmon fillets (about 1-inch thick)
1 lemon
1/2 tsp Italian seasoning

1. Preheat oven to 450°F with racks in upper and lower thirds of the oven. Line 2 rimmed baking sheets with foil and spray with nonstick cooking spray.
2. Meanwhile, in a large bowl, add eggplant, bell pepper, squash, onion, tomatoes, oil, 3/4 tsp salt and 1/4 tsp pepper; tossing well. Divide mixture between the prepared baking sheets and roast on the upper and lower racks, stirring once halfway through cooking, 25 minutes or until the vegetables are tender and lightly browned.
3. Return vegetables to the large bowl and stir in capers, vinegar and honey. Set aside.
4. Grate lemon zest and measure 1 tsp. Cut the remaining lemon into wedges and set aside.
5. Place salmon on one of the baking sheets. Sprinkle salmon with zest, Italian seasoning and the remaining salt and pepper.
6. Place pan on the lower rack and roast 9 minutes or until the salmon is opaque and flakes easily when tested with a fork.
7. Transfer salmon to serving plates and spoon the caponata alongside. Serve with the lemon wedges

Salmon Provençal with Fennel and Orange

Salmon is uniquely seasoned with a blend of herbs, fennel, and orange zest to create a mouth-watering dish, then seared and broiled to flaky, moist perfection.

Makes 4 Servings

Calories 328 | Carbohydrate 15 g | Fiber 1 g | Fat 17 g | Protein 30 g

4 skin-on salmon fillets (about 5 oz each)
Kosher salt
Freshly ground black pepper
1 tbsp fennel seed, ground
1 tbsp herbs de Provence
1 tbsp orange zest
2 tbsp olive oil

1. Preheat oven to 400°F.
2. Season salmon with salt and pepper. In a small bowl, combine ground fennel, herbs de Provence and orange zest. Press mixture into the top of the salmon.
3. In a large ovenproof nonstick skillet over medium-high heat add the oil and heat until shimmering. Place salmon seasoned-side down in the skillet. Cook, 1 minute or until the spice mixture is nicely browned. Turn salmon over and cook 1 minutes more.
4. Transfer skillet to oven and cook, 7 minutes or until salmon is opaque and flakes easily with a fork.

Salmon with Sun-Dried Tomato Couscous

With one single pan, you can turn salmon, sun dried tomatoes, and couscous into a divinely healthy evening meal.

Makes 4 Servings

Calories 524 | Carbohydrate 36 g | Fiber 4 g | Fat 26 g | Protein 36 g

1 lemon
1 1/4 lbs skinless salmon, cut into 4 pieces
1/4 cup sun-dried tomato pesto, divided
Kosher salt
Freshly ground black pepper
2 tbsp virgin olive oil, divided
1 cup couscous
3 green onions, sliced
1-1/2 cups low-sodium chicken broth
2 cloves garlic, chopped
2 tbsp pine nuts, toasted

1. Zest lemon and reserve the zest. Cut the lemon into 8 slices. Brush 1-1/2 tsp pesto on each salmon piece. Season with salt and pepper.
2. In a large skillet over medium-high heat, add 1 tbsp oil and heat until shimmering. Add couscous and onions; cook, stirring often, 2 minutes or until the couscous is lightly toasted, Stir in broth, lemon zest and garlic.
3. Arrange the salmon on top of the couscous, pressing down gently to cover the bottom and sides of the salmon. Arrange lemon slices on top of salmon.
4. Reduce heat to medium-low. Cover and cook 12 minutes or until the salmon is opaque and flakes easily with a fork and the couscous is tender.
5. Using a spatula, transfer salmon to serving plates. Ladle couscous around salmon. Serve garnished with toasted pine nuts.

Baked Lump Crab Cakes

Create mouthwatering crab cakes with rich lump crab meat and no fillers. Baking the crab cakes gives them a fluffy mounded shape of wonderfully seasoned crabmeat with a heart-healthy cooking method.

Makes 6 Servings

Calories 234 | Carbohydrate 5 g | Fiber 1 g | Fat 15 g | Protein 19 g

1 lemon, cut into 8 wedges
1 egg
1/2 cup real mayonnaise
1 tsp Worcestershire sauce
1 tsp Dijon mustard
1 tsp seafood seasoning, preferably Old Bay
1/4 tspcayenne pepper
Pinch kosher salt
1-1/2 lbs lump crab meat
1/4 cup chopped fresh parsley
2 green onions, thinly sliced
1/2 cup Panko bread crumbs
Pickled red onions
Watercress
Mandarin orange slices (optional)

1. Line a baking sheet with parchment paper. Set aside.
2. In a large bowl, squeeze 1 tsp lemon juice (about 2 lemon wedges). Set aside the remaining lemon wedges.
3. In the same bowl, whisk in the egg, mayonnaise, Worcestershire sauce, mustard, seafood seasoning, cayenne and salt. Gently stir in crab, parsley and onions. Fold in bread crumbs until just combined.
4. Gently form crab mixture into 12 balls, without squeezing, and arrange on prepared baking sheet. Gently press balls into thick patties. Refrigerate for 30 minutes.
5. Preheat oven to 400°F.
6. Bake crab cakes for 12 to 15 minutes or until the tops are light golden brown and an instant-read thermometer registers 165° F.
7. Transfer to serving plates. Serve garnished with lemon wedges, pickled onions, watercress, and orange slices (if using).

Lemon Garlic Baked Cod

The flavor, texture and melt-in-your-mouth appeal of cod is highlighted by a spicy harissa-style mixture of herbs.

Makes 4 Servings

Calories 280 | Carbohydrate 5 g | Fiber 2 g | Fat 15 g | Protein 31 g

4 6-oz pieces cod fillets
Kosher salt
Freshly ground black
    pepper
2 lemons
3 tbsp virgin olive oil
3 cloves garlic, minced
1 tsp paprika
1 tsp ground coriander
3/4 tsp ground cumin
1/8 tsp cayenne pepper
1/4 cup chopped fresh
    parsley leaves

1. Preheat oven to 400°F with a rack in the middle of the oven.
2. Brush cod fillet with olive oil and arrange in a 9-by 13-inch glass baking dish with space inbetween. Season with salt and pepper.
3. Squeeze 4 tbsp lemon juice and grate 1/2 tsp zest from lemons. Cut the remaining lemon into wedges. Set aside.
4. In a small saucepan over medium heat, add the remaining oil and heat until shimmering. Add the garlic and cook, stirring, 30 seconds or until fragrant. Remove from the heat and stir in the lemon juice, paprika, coriander, cumin and cayenne. Pour mixture over fillets.
4. Bake, basting occasionally, 10 to 15 minutes or until the fish is opaque and flakes easily when tested with a fork.
5. Transfer fillets to serving plates and spoon liquids from the baking dish over the top. Sprinkle with parsley. Serve garnished with the lemon wedges.

Swordfish with Tarragon Caper Sauce

This tangy sauce balances the distinct taste of swordfish. This steak-from-the-sea is a delightful treat when drizzled with this tarragon caper sauce

Makes 4 Servings

Calories 378 | Carbohydrate 5 g | Fiber 1 g | Fat 20 g | Protein 28 g

3 tbsp virgin olive oil
4 5-oz skinless
    swordfish fillets
    (about 1-inch-thick)
Kosher salt
Freshly ground black
    pepper
1 small yellow onion,
    diced
1 clove garlic, minced
1 tsp dried tarragon
1/2 tsp paprika
3/4 cup dry white wine
2 tbsp capers, rinsed
    and drained
1 tsp fresh lemon juice
2 tbsp chopped fresh
    parsley

1. In a large heavy-bottom skillet over medium-high heat, add 1-1/2 tbsp oil and heat until shimmering. Season fillets with salt and pepper. Cook, turning once, 7 to 9 minutes or until the fish is opaque. Transfer to a plate and cover to keep warm.

2. Reduce the heat to medium. Add the remaining oil to the skillet and heat until shimmering. Add the onion and cook, stirring occasionally, 3 minutes or until softened. Add the garlic and cook, stirring, 1 minute or until fragrant. Stir in the wine, tarragon and paprika and heat until boiling. Reduce heat to medium-low and cook, stirring occasionally, about 3 minutes or until the liquid is reduced by half.

3. Add the capers and lemon juice; cook, stirring, 2 minutes. Stir in the parsley.

4. Transfer swordfish to serving plates. Serve drizzled with sauce.

Baked Tuna Steaks with Garlic Aioli

A chilled creamy garlic aioli is the perfect topping for these baked tuna steaks. When served with a fresh mixed green salad you have a healthy satisfying meal.

Makes 4 Servings

Calories 371 | Carbohydrate 2 g | Fiber 0 g | Fat 25 g | Protein 34 g

Aioli
2 cloves garlic, smashed
1/2 cup Greek yogurt
2 tbsp extra virgin olive
   oil
1 tbsp fresh lemon juice
Kosher salt
Freshly ground black
   pepper
Tuna
2 tbsp chopped fresh
   basil
1/4 cup virgin olive oil
1/4 tsp garlic powder
4 tuna steaks, 1 inch
   thick (about 5 oz
   each)

Tip
* Aioli can be made up to 1
   day ahead of time.

1. Preheat oven to 450°F.
2. *Aioli:* Using a mortar and pestle, mash garlic and 1/4 tsp salt until a paste.
2. In a small bowl, add yogurt, oil, juice and garlic paste, whisking until blended. Season to taste with salt and pepper. Cover and refrigerate.
3. *Tuna:* In another small bowl, add basil, oil and garlic powder. Season with salt and pepper.
4. Line a rimmed baking sheet with foil. Brush tuna with basil oil mixture. Bake tuna 8 to 12 minutes or until tuna flakes easily when tested with a fork but is lightly pink in the middle.
5. Transfer tuna to serving plates. Serve with a large dollop of aioli.

Variation:
* Replace the Aioli with Cucumber Lemon Relish. The calories are reduced by approximately 60 kcals, while the percentage balance of other nutrients remains about the same with the fat grams about 20% lower.

Cucumber Lemon Relish: In a medium bowl, toss together the 1 finely diced seedless cucumber, 2 tbsp lemon juice and 1/2 tsp granulated sugar. Season to taste with salt and pepper. Stir in 1/4 extra virgin olive oil, 2 tbsp minced fresh dill and 1 tbsp minced shallots. Let stand 30 minutes. After 30 minutes, season to taste with salt and pepper. Serve dolloped on the tuna steaks.

Easy Smothered Baked Tilapia

Indulge yourself in this quick and easy to prepare meal of tilapia smothered in tomatoes, artichokes, and kalamata olives.

Makes 4 Servings

Calories 202 | Carbohydrate 6 g | Fiber 2 g | Fat 6 g | Protein 31 g

4 5-oz tilapia filets
Kosher salt
Freshly ground black
   pepper
2/3 cup canned diced
   Italian tomatoes,
   drained
1/3 cup coarsely
   chopped artichoke
   hearts
1/3 cup sliced kalamata
   olives
1⁄3 cup crumbled feta
   cheese

1. Preheat oven to 400°.
2. Spray a 13- by 9-inch glass baking dish with nonstick cooking spray. Arrange filets in dish, with space in between each filet. Season fish with salt and pepper. Top with tomatoes, artichoke hearts and olives.
3. Bake 10 minutes and then sprinkle with cheese. Continue baking 5 more minutes or until fish is opaque and flakes easily when tested with a fork.
4. Transfer to serving plates. Serve immediately.

Tip
*   You can purchase small quantities of artichoke hearts and kalamata olives at the salad bar of your grocery store.

Steamed Mussels with Tomatoes and Olives

Mussels are a true favorite when cooked with this spiced blend of vegetables and herbs.

Makes 4 Servings

Calories 358 | Carbohydrate 23 g | Fiber 4 g | Fat 15 g | Protein 33 g

2 tbsp virgin olive oil
2 medium onions, sliced
4 cloves garlic, minced
1/2 tsp paprika
Pinch cayenne pepper
Kosher salt
1 can (14.5 oz) diced
tomatoes, drained
1 cup water
2-1/4 lbs mussels,
scrubbed
2/3 cup halved pitted
green olives
1/2 cup roughly
chopped fresh
parsley

Serving Suggestion
* Serve with loaves of crusty French bread for dipping in the liquids.

1. In a large Dutch oven over medium heat, add the oil and heat until shimmering. Add the onions and cook, stirring often, 7 minutes or until softened and golden brown. Add the garlic and cook, stirring, 1 minute or until fragrant. Stir in the paprika, cayenne pepper, 1-1/2 tsp salt, tomatoes and 1 cup water; cook, scraping up any browned bits from the bottom of the pot, until simmering.
2. Add the mussels, olives and parsley. Cover and cook 5 to 7 minutes or until the mussels are opened. Discard any unopened mussels.
3. Spoon into individual serving bowls. Serve immediately.

Sheetpan Mediterranean Shrimp

You will enjoy this healthy weeknight dinner that is easy to make and delightfully satisfying. Additionally, you have a complete meal in one-pot.

Makes 4 Servings

Calories 527 | Carbohydrate 44 g | Fiber 10 g | Fat 23 g | Protein 40 g

1-1/2 lbs Yukon Gold potatoes, peeled and sliced 1/2 inch thick

2 fennel bulbs, cut into 1-inch thick wedges

3 tbsp virgin olive oil (approx.), divided

Kosher salt

Freshly ground black pepper

1 lemon

2 lbs peeled and deveined jumbo shrimp (16/20 count), tails removed

1 tsp grated lemon zest, plus lemon wedges for serving

2 tsp dried oregano

1 cup crumbled feta cheese

1/2 cup pitted kalamata olives, halved

2 tbsp chopped fresh parsley

1. Preheat oven to 450°F with oven rack in lower third of oven.
2. In a medium bowl, add potatoes, fennel, 2 tbsp oil, 1 tsp salt and 1/4 tsp pepper, tossing to coat. Line a rimmed baking sheet with foil. Arrange vegetables on sheet. Bake 25 minutes or until just tender.
3. Grate 1 tsp lemon zest. Cut the remaining lemon into wedges. Set aside.
4. Rinse shrimp and pat dry. In a medium bowl, add shrimp, zest, oregano, the remaining oil, 1/2 tsp salt and 1/4 tsp pepper, tossing well to coat.
5. Turn over roasted vegetables. Place shrimp on top of vegetables. Sprinkle feta over the top. Bake 7 minutes or until shrimp are pink firm and opaque.
6. Sprinkle with olives and parsley. Drizzle with olive oil.
7. Transfer to serving plates. Serve garnished with lemon wedges.

Braised Shrimp, Bell Peppers and Tomatoes

Shrimp prepared with fresh tomatoes and green bell peppers turn this recipe into is large and filling Mediterranean meal.

Makes 4 Servings

Calories 307 | Carbohydrate 11 g | Fiber 3 g | Fat 15 g | Protein 25 g

1-1/2 lbs extra-large peeled and deveined shrimp (21/30 count)
1/4 cup extra-virgin olive oil, divided
2 tsp anise extract
5 garlic cloves, minced
1 tsp grated zest from 1 lemon
Kosher salt
Freshly ground black pepper
1 small onion, diced
1 medium green bell pepper, stemmed, seeded, and diced
1/2 tsp red pepper flakes
1 can (28-oz) diced tomato, 1/3 cup juices reserved
1/4 cup dry white wine
2 tbsp coarsely chopped fresh parsley leaves
Chopped fresh basil leaves
2 tbsp chopped fresh dill leaves

1. In a large bowl, add shrimp, 1 tbsp oil, 1 tsp anise, 1 tsp garlic, lemon zest, 1/4 tsp salt and 1/8 tsp pepper tossing until well combined. Set aside.
2. In a large skillet over medium heat, add 2 tbsp oil and heat until shimmering. Add onion, bell pepper and 1/4 tsp salt; cook, stirring occasionally 7 to 9 minutes or until vegetable are softened. Add remaining garlic and red pepper flakes; cook, stirring 1 minute or until fragrant. Add tomatoes and reserved juice, wine, and remaining anise; increase heat to medium-high and bring to a simmer. Reduce heat to medium and simmer, stirring occasionally, 7 to 9 minutes or until sauce is slightly thickened. Stir in parsley. Season to taste with salt and pepper.
3. Reduce heat to medium-low. Add shrimp and any accumulated juices, stirring well. Cover and cook, stirring occasionally, 7 to 9 minutes or until shrimp are pink, firm and opaque.
4. Transfer to serving bowls and drizzle with remaining olive oil. Serve garnished with basil.

Marinated Shrimp and Vegetable Kabobs

Shrimp and colorful vegetables become a filling and delicious main entrée when marinated with this exceptional dressing. As mouthwatering to behold as it is to eat.

Makes 4 Servings

Calories 524 | Carbohydrate 20 g | Fiber 4 g | Fat 42 g | Protein 19 g

Eight 12-in bamboo
  skewers
2 lemons
1/4 cup extra-virgin
  olive oil
1/4 cup red wine
  vinegar
2 cloves garlic, minced
1-1/2 tsp Kosher salt
3/4 tsp freshly ground
  black pepper
1 lb large peeled
  uncooked shrimp
24 cherry tomatoes
2 green bell peppers,
  cored and cut into 24
  pieces
24 large pearl onions,
  peeled

Tip
* Heat the reserved
  marinade in a small
  saucepan over medium-
  low heat and drizzle over
  shrimp. Or if serving with
  a rice side dish, drizzle
  warm marinade over rice.

1. Preheat oven to 400°F.
2. Place bamboo skewers into a tray and cover with water. Set aside.
3. Squeeze 3 tbsp lemon juice into a small bowl. Cut the remaining lemon into wedges and set aside.
4. In the small bowl with the juice, whisk in the oil, vinegar, garlic, salt and pepper.
5. In a large resealable plastic bag, add the shrimp and 1 cup marinade, tossing to coat. Set aside remaining marinade. Refrigerate shrimp for 30 minutes to 1 hour, turning often.
6. Remove the shrimp from the marinade. (see tip) Thread the shrimp, tomatoes, peppers and onions, alternating until each skewer is filled but with a little space between each item.
7. Spray a large rimmed baking sheet with nonstick cooked spray. Arrange the skewers on the tray and brush with the reserved marinade. Roast shrimp 5 to 7 minutes or until shrimp are pink, firm and opaque.
8. Transfer to serving plates, removing from skewers if desired. Serve immediately.

FISH AND SEAFOOD

Date and Walnut Stuffed Chicken Breast

A quick and easy way to make a chicken entrée bursting with Mediterranean flavors and aromas.

Makes 2 Servings

Calories 617 | Carbohydrate 33 g | Fiber 5 g | Fat 34 g | Protein 41 g

2 tbsp virgin olive oil
1/2 cup chopped onion
1/4 cup dates
    (preferably Medjool),
    pitted and chopped
1/4 cup chopped pecans
1 tbsp finely chopped
    rosemary leaves
1/2 cup finely shredded
    parmesan
Kosher salt and freshly
    ground pepper
2 boneless skinless
    chicken breasts
    (about 5 oz each)
1/4 cup dry white wine,
    such as Pinot Grigio

Tip
*   You can substitute chicken
    broth for the white wine if
    desired

1. Preheat oven to 400°F.
2. In a medium saucepan over medium heat, add oil and heat until shimmering. Add the onions and cook 3 to 5 minutes or until soft.
3. Stir in the dates, pecans, rosemary and parmesan. Season with salt and pepper. Set aside.
4. Cut a slit horizontally into the thickest part of the breasts to make a pocket; do not cut completely through the breasts.
5. Spoon mixture into each of the pockets packing filling tightly.
6. Transfer breasts to a square glass baking dish. Pour wine around chicken. Season chicken with salt.
7. Bake 30 minutes or until an instant-read thermometer inserted into the thickest part of the breast registers 165° and the chicken is no longer pink in the middle. Serve immediately.

Mediterranean Stuffed Chicken

Tasty vegetables enhanced with herbs and spices will make this one of your favorite easy to make Mediterranean entrées.

Makes 3 Servings

Calories 393 | Carbohydrate 14 g | Fiber 4 g | Fat 25 g | Protein 28 g

1/3 cup crumbled feta cheese

3 sun dried tomatoes (in oil), drained and diced

3 tbsp finely chopped walnuts

4 black olives, (preferably Kalamata) chopped

1 lemon, zest and juice

2 tsp ground oregano

2 boneless skinless chicken breasts, (about 5 oz each)

8 fresh basil leaves

1 tsp extra-virgin olive oil

Kosher salt and freshly ground black pepper

Tip
* Chicken rollups can be prepared ahead of time. Store in an airtight container in the refrigerator up to 2 days. Add 5 to 10 minutes to cooking time.

1. Preheat oven to 400°F.
2. In a small bowl, combine the feta cheese, tomatoes, walnuts, olives, 2 tsp lemon zest, 2 tsp lemon juice and oregano. Set aside.
3. Place chicken breasts between 2 sheets of plastic wrap. Using a mallet, pound chicken to 1/2 inch thick.
4. Place 3 to 4 basil leaves on each breast, leaving 1/2-inch space from edges.
5. Spoon half of cheese mixture in the center of each breast.
6. Starting with the narrower end, roll up the breast up tightly. Use 2 to 3 toothpicks to secure rolls. Brush rollups with oil. Season with salt and pepper
7. Bake for 25 minutes or until an instant-read thermometer inserted into the thickest part registers 165° and chicken is no longer pink inside.

Chicken, Feta and Kalamata Wraps

This is a quick and tasty meal packed full of Mediterranean flavor that can be easily made using a ready-made rotisserie chicken.

Makes 6 servings

Calories 373 | Carbohydrate 21 g | Fiber 2 g | Fat 16 g | Protein 39 g

1 rotisserie chicken, about 2-1/2 lbs, shredded

4 ozs feta cheese, crumbled

1/2 cup roasted red peppers, coarsely chopped

1/2 cup pitted kalamata olives, coarsely chopped

2 tbsp minced shallot

1 tsp lemon zest

2 tsps lemon juice

1/2 tsp kosher salt

1/4 tsp freshly ground black pepper

1/2 cup plain fat free Greek yogurt

4 large flour tortillas (12-inch diameter

4 ozs arugula (about 4 cups)

1. In a large bowl, combine chicken, feta, red peppers, olives, shallot, zest, juice, salt, pepper and yogurt.
2. Arrange tortillas on work service. Divide arugula in the middle of each tortilla. Spoon one-quarter chicken mixture on top of the arugula. Roll tortilla up tightly, tucking in one edge as you roll.
3. Wraps can be eaten immediately or tightly covered in plastic wrap and refrigerated for up to 2 days.

Paella Valenciana

Mediterranean cooking at its best with chicken, shrimp, and Italian sausage smothered in a tasty balance of rice, vegetables, herbs, and spices.

Makes 8 Servings

Calories 517 | Carbohydrate 38 g | Fiber 3 g | Fat 15 g | Protein 59 g

3 tbsp virgin olive oil
1 whole chicken, about 3 lbs, cut into 8 pieces
1 small onion cut into 1/8-inch slices
4 medium tomatoes, each cut into 6 wedges
1 tbsp paprika
1 tbsp kosher salt
1/2 tsp freshly ground black pepper
1/4 tsp cayenne pepper
3 saffron threads
1-1/2 cups arborio rice
3 cups chicken broth
1 lb large (31/35 count) shrimp, peeled and deveined
1-1/2 cups frozen peas
1 jar (4 oz) sliced pimiento, drained

1. In a large Dutch oven or Paella pan over medium heat, add 2 tbsp oil and heat until shimmering. Working in batches, add chicken and cook, turning, 6 to 8 minutes or until browned all over. Transfer chicken to a plate, adding oil as necessary between batches.
2. Add onions and tomatoes to the Dutch oven; cook, stirring often, 5 minutes or until onion is softened.
3. Stir in paprika, salt, black pepper, cayenne pepper, saffron, rice and broth. Add chicken, cover and simmer 20 minutes.
4. Gently stir in shrimp and peas. Cook, stirring often, 10 minutes or until shrimp are pink, firm and opaque and peas are tender. Gently stir in pimiento and cook until heated through. Serve immediately.

Variations
* You can omit the shrimp, if you prefer.
* Add 1 lb white fish fillets, cut into 2 inch chunks with the shrimp in step 4.

Roman Chicken with Peppers

Colorful bell peppers and tomatoes infused with wine and herbs give loads of taste and character to chicken thighs

Makes 4 Servings

Calories 401 | Carbohydrate 7 g | Fiber 2 g | Fat 16 g | Protein 46 g

2 tbsp virgin olive oil
8 skinless boneless
   chicken thighs
Kosher salt and freshly
   ground black pepper
1 yellow bell pepper, cut
   into 1/2 inch slices
2 cloves garlic, minced
1 tbsp chopped thyme
1 tbsp chopped oregano
1 cup dry white wine
1 can (15 oz) diced
   tomatoes
1/2 cup chicken broth
2 tbsp capers
1/2 cup chopped parsley

1. In a large skillet over medium-high heat add the oil and heat until shimmering. Season chicken with salt and pepper. Working in batches, cook the thighs, turning once, 6 minutes or until browned all over. Transfer to a plate and repeat with remaining thighs, adding more oil as necessary.
2. Reduce heat to medium. Add the peppers and cook, stirring often, 5 minutes or until tender Add the garlic and cook, stirring, 1 minute or until fragrant.
3. Stir in the thyme, oregano and wine; cook, scraping up any browned bits from the bottom of the skillet, 5 minutes.
4. Stir in the tomatoes and broth. Return the chicken to the skillet. Cover and cook, 15 to 20 minutes or until an instant-read thermometer inserted into the thickest part of the thigh registers 165° and the juices run clear when pierced with a fork.
5. Stir in the capers and parsley. Serve immediately.

Chicken Artichoke and Tomato Casserole

This delicious casserole is bursting with flavors and aromas produced from a delicate combination of roasted chicken, tasty vegetables, olives, white wine, and orange juice.

Makes 8 Servings

Calories 403 | Carbohydrate 13 g | Fiber 4 g | Fat 26 g | Protein 32 g

2 packages (9 oz) frozen artichoke hearts, thawed and drained
1/4 cup virgin olive oil
Kosher salt and freshly ground black pepper
8 bone-in, skin-on chicken breasts, (about 4 oz each)
1 large onion, minced
2 tsp minced fresh thyme leaves
6 garlic cloves, minced
1/2 cup dry white wine
1/2 cup orange juice
2 cans (14.5 oz) diced tomatoes
1 tbsp tomato paste
1 cup kalamata olives, pitted and coarsely chopped
2 tbsp chopped fresh parsley leaves

> Tip
> * You can substitute an 18 oz can or jar of artichoke hearts in water for the frozen artichokes. Do not use artichokes that have been marinated in oil.

1. Preheat oven to 450°.
2. In a medium bowl, add artichokes, 2 tbsp oil, 1/2 tsp salt and 1/4 tsp pepper; toss gently to combine.. Spread mixture into an 8-by 13-inch baking dish and roast, 20 to 25 minutes or until the edges are browned. Set aside.
3. Season chicken with salt and pepper. In a large skillet over medium-high heat add 1 tbsp oil and heat until shimmering. Working in batches, add chicken, skin-side down, and cook 8 minutes or until brown. Transfer chicken to a plate and repeat.
4. Adjust heat to medium, add remaining oil to the skillet and heat until shimmering. Add the onion and thyme; cook, stirring often, 7 minutes or until onion is golden. Add garlic and cook, stirring, 1 minute or fragrant.
6. Stir in the wine and juice; cook, stirring and scraping up any brown bits, 8 minutes or until reduced by half. Add the tomatoes and paste; cook, stirring often, 5 minutes or until the sauce is slightly thickened. Stir in the olives.
7. Stir sauce into the artichokes. Arrange chicken, skin side up, in between the artichokes. Bake 30 minutes, or until the chicken is no longer pink inside and an instant-read thermometer registers 165° when inserted into the thickest part of the breast. Remove from oven and let stand 5 minutes. Serve immediately

Chicken, Peppers and Red Onion Kabobs

Tender chunks of chicken are marinated with herbs and spices and prepared with complimentary vegetables for a simply ideal Mediterranean meal.

Makes 6 Servings

Calories 410 | Carbohydrate 6 g | Fiber 1 g | Fat 25 g | Protein 39 g

3 large cloves garlic, crushed

3 tbsp finely chopped fresh rosemary leaves

1-1/2 tbsp finely chopped fresh oregano

2 tsp kosher salt

1/2 tsp freshly ground black pepper

6 tbsp olive oil

1/4 cup fresh lemon juice

1-1/2 lb boneless skinless chicken breasts, cut into 1 inch pieces

1 red bell pepper, cut into 1 inch pieces

1 red onion, cut into 1 inch wedges

1. In a large bowl, combine garlic, rosemary, oregano, 1 tsp salt, pepper, 5 tbsp oil and 3 tbsp juice. Add chicken, tossing to coat in marinade. Cover and refrigerate 30 minutes or up to an hour.

2. Meanwhile soak wooden skewer in water for about 30 minutes.

3. Preheat oven to 425°F.

4. In a small bowl, combine remaining lemon juice, oil and salt. Thread chicken, peppers and onions onto skewers, alternating as desired. Discard marinade.

5. Arrange skewers on a foil-lined baking sheet with a rack. Baste skewer with lemon mixture. Bake, turning occasionally and basting with lemon mixture, 12 minutes or until chicken is no longer pink in the middle and vegetables are tender. Discard remaining lemon mixture.

Chicken Souvlaki with Tzatziki Sauce

Bring this simple and delicious Mediterranean entrée to your table loaded with broiled chicken and topped with creamy tzatziki sauce.

Makes 4 Servings

Calories 344 | Carbohydrate 8 g | Fiber 1 g | Fat 17 g | Protein 39 g

1/4 cup virgin olive oil
3 tbsp fresh lemon juice
2 cloves garlic, minced
2 tsp chopped fresh oregano
3/4 tsp kosher salt
1/4 tsp freshly ground black pepper
4 tbsp red wine vinegar
4 boneless skinless chicken breasts, cut into 1-1/2 inch wide strips)

Tzatziki Sauce

1 medium cucumber, peeled and sliced
Kosher salt
Freshly ground black pepper
2 cloves garlic, minced
1/3 cup chopped dill, fresh
2 cups plain fat free Greek yogurt
1-1/2 tbsp fresh lemon juice

1. In a large bowl, whisk together, oil, juice, garlic, oregano, salt, pepper and vinegar. Add chicken, tossing to coat in marinade. Cover and refrigerate 30 minutes or up to 1 hour.
2. Meanwhile, soak wooden skewers in cold water.
3. *Tzatziki Sauce:* Add cucumbers to a colander and sprinkle generously with salt. Let cucumbers drain for 30 minutes, tossing occasionally.
4. Add cucumber, garlic, dill, yogurt and lemon juice to a blender. Season with pepper. Blend until smooth and creamy. Transfer to a bowl, cover and refrigerate.
5. Preheat oven to 425°F.
6. Remove chicken from marinade and thread onto skewers. Discard marinade.
7. Arrange skewers on a foil-lined baking sheet with a rack. Bake 7 to 9 minutes, turning once, or until chicken is no longer pink in the middle. Transfer to serving plates.
8. Serve with tzatziki sauce on the side for dipping.

Easy Weeknight Tandoori Chicken

Craving wonderfully marinated chicken thighs that will make you swoon with delight? Then these tender and moist boneless chicken thighs with a delightfully crispy outside are the right choice.

Makes 4 Servings

Calories 384 | Carbohydrate 9 g | Fiber 1 g | Fat 19 g | Protein 44 g

2 cups Greek yogurt
4 tsp minced garlic
4 tsp paprika
4 tsp ground coriander
2 tsp ground cumin
2 tsp minced ginger
1 tsp red pepper flakes
Lime, juice of
Kosher salt
Freshly ground black
    pepper
1-1/2 lbs boneless,
    skinless chicken
    thighs
Chopped fresh cilantro

Tips
* Serve with a side of
  Basmati rice and drizzle
  the remaining yogurt
  mixture over the top.
* Serve with sautéed spinach
  on the side.

1. In a large bowl, combine yogurt, garlic, paprika, coriander, cumin, ginger, red pepper flakes and half the lime juice. Dredge chicken in yogurt mixture. Cover and let stand 30 minutes.
2. Preheat broiler.
3. Line a rimmed baking sheet with aluminum foil. Transfer chicken breast to pan, bottom-side up. Reserve marinade.
4. Broil 3 to 4 minutes or until lightly browned. Turn chicken over and pour remaining marinade over the top. Broil 3 to 4 minutes or until lightly browned on the top.
5. Drizzle remaining lime juice over chicken. Transfer to serving plates. Spoon some of the cooked yogurt mixture over the chicken. Garnish with cilantro. Serve remaining yogurt mixture on the side.

Braised Chicken Breasts with Bulgur Pilaf

Serving this pan-seared chicken breast with these savory ingredients will bring out the best of Mediterranean cuisine.

Makes 4 Servings

Calories 403 | Carbohydrate 13 g | Fiber 4 g | Fat 26 g | Protein 32 g

4 boneless, skinless
   chicken breasts,
   about 5 oz each
Kosher salt and freshly
   ground black pepper
1/3 cup virgin olive oil
1 cup fine-grind bulgur
10 ozs cherry tomatoes,
   halved
1/2 cup pitted kalamata
   olives, halved
4 ozs feta cheese,
   crumbled
3/4 cup minced fresh
   parsley
1 tbsp fresh lemon juice

1. Season chicken with salt and pepper. In a large skillet over medium-high heat, add 1 tbsp oil and heat until shimmering. Cook breasts, turning once, 8 minutes or until browned and no longer pink in the middle. Transfer chicken to cutting board and tent with foil.

2. Add 1-1/2 cups water to the skillet and cook, scraping up any browned bits from the bottom of the pan, until mixture begins to boil. Stir in 2 tsp salt and bulgur. Remove from the heat. Cover and an let stand 5 minutes, or until bulgur is al dente.

3. Fluff bulgur with a fork. Stir in tomatoes, olives, feta, parsley, lemon juice and 2 tbsp oil. Season to taste with salt and pepper.

4. Slice chicken across the grain. Spoon bulgur onto serving plates. Arrange chicken on and around bulgur. Serve drizzled with remaining oil.

MEATS

Herb Roasted Lamb Chops

Not only is this dish incredibly easy to prepare, but it tastes incredible too. Thick lamb chops are graced with garlic and rosemary for a tender, juicy, and delicious entrée. Make it for guests or enjoy it for an easy weeknight meal.

Makes 4 Servings

Calories 498 | Carbohydrate 1 g | Fiber 0 g | Fat 39 g | Protein 36 g

3 tbsp extra-virgin olive oil
8 lamb chops
2 cloves garlic, cut into small slices
Kosher salt
2 tbsp fresh rosemary leaves

Tip
* When cutting the slit into your lamb chops, make sure you do not cut all the way through the chop.

1. Preheat oven to 375°F.
2. Place chops on rack in a baking sheet. Brush chops with olive oil. Cut 1 small, shallow slit in the top of each lamb chop. Place a sliver of garlic in each cut. Season lamb with salt and sprinkle with rosemary.
3. Roast chops 20 minutes or until an instant-read thermometer inserted in the thickest part of the chop registers 160°F for medium. Serve warm.

Braised Lamb Shanks

You will need to plan-ahead to make these delectable lamb shanks, but the results are worth it. When marinating overnight in a Persian-inspired combination of spices, the lamb takes on a whole new depth of flavor. You can make the dish up to 2 days ahead of time – just reheat and serve. This certainly is a company-worthy dish that is so easy to reheat and serve on the day of your dinner party. You can easily double this recipe.

Makes 8 Servings

Calories 522 | Carbohydrate 7 g | Fiber 2 g | Fat 35 g | Protein 44 g

4 meaty lamb shanks (about 4 1/2 lbs), trimmed
Kosher salt
2 tsp ground cinnamon
1 tsp grated nutmeg
1 tsp ground cardamom
1 tsp freshly ground black pepper
1 tsp turmeric
Vegetable oil
4 tsp crumbled saffron
2 limes, zest and juice of
1 large onion roughly chopped
1 orange, zest of
3 fresh thyme sprigs
2 bay leaves
6 cups hot chicken broth or water
2 tbsp coarsely chopped parsley
2 tbsp coarsely chopped dill

1. Season shanks with salt. In a small bowl, combine cinnamon, nutmeg, cardamom, black pepper and turmeric. Sprinkle mixture over shanks and rub in. Wrap shanks in plastic wrap and refrigerate 8 hours or overnight.

2. In a large Dutch oven over medium-high heat, add 1/2 inch of oil and heat until shimmering. Working in batches, add lamb shanks and cook, turning frequently, 5 minutes or until browned all over. Transfer to a plate and repeat with remaining shanks.

3. Meanwhile, in a small bowl combine saffron, lime juice and 1/2 cup warm water. Set aside.

4. Preheat oven to 350°F.

5. Discard all but 2 tbsp oil from the Dutch oven. Over medium heat add onion and cook, stirring often, 7 to 9 minutes or until softened and lightly browned. Season onion with salt. Stir in zest of 1 lime, orange zest, thyme. bay leaves and saffron mixture. Arrange shanks in the Dutch oven and pour in broth. Heating until boiling.

(continued on next page)

Braised Lamb Shanks (continued)

6. Cover pot and bake for about 1 1/2 hours or until an instant-read thermometer registers 160°F when inserted into the thickest part of the shank for medium and meat is beginning to fall off the bone.

7. Transfer shanks to a large shallow dish and cover with foil. Strain liquid through a fine-mesh sieve into a small saucepan. Discard onions, thyme and bay leaves. Skim fat from liquids. Season to taste with salt. Cook juices over medium heat until warmed through.

8. Meanwhile, remove lamb from bones and break into large chunks. Discard bones. Transfer lamb to individual wide serving bowls. Ladle juices into bowls. Serve garnished with parsley and dill.

Sirloin Ribbons

These marinated thin slices of sirloin are great just about anytime. Serve them as a main course or as an appetizer.

Makes 4 Servings

Calories 342 | Carbohydrate 2 g | Fiber 0 g | Fat 17 g | Protein 47 g

1-1/4 lbs sirloin steak, cut into 1/4 inch thick strips.
3 cloves garlic, mashed
2 tsp dried oregano
2 tsp kosher salt
1/2 tsp freshly ground black pepper
1 tbsp virgin olive oil
1 tbsp red wine vinegar

1. In a 11-by 7-inch glass baking dish, add the garlic, oregano, salt, pepper, oil and vinegar, mixing well.
2. Add the steak strips, tossing to coat in marinade. Cover and refrigerate for about 2 hours.
3. Meanwhile, soak wooden skewers in water for about 30 minutes.
4. Preheat broiler with oven rack 5 inches from the top.
5. Weave steak onto skewers. Arrange skewers on a foil-lined baking sheet with a rack.
6. Broil, turning once, about 3 minutes or until nicely browned.
7. Transfer skewer to plates and serve immediately.

Provençal Beef Daube

This classic French beef stew is a one-pot wonder of pure comfort food. It can be made ahead of time and freezes well.

Makes 8 Servings

Calories 457 | Carbohydrate 12 g | Fiber 3 g | Fat 28 g | Protein 24 g

2 lbs beef top round roast or chuck roast, cut into 2-inch cubes
4 tbsp virgin olive oil
2 tbsp brandy
Kosher salt
Freshly ground black pepper
4 carrots, cut into 1/2-inch slices
2 onions, thinly sliced
4 oz button mushrooms, sliced
1 medium head of garlic (about 10 to 12 cloves), separated, peeled and smashed
1 orange, zest of
2 tomatoes, chopped
1 bottle dry white wine or dry vermouth
12 sprigs of fresh parsley
8 sprigs fresh thyme
2 bay leaves
1/2 tsp black peppercorns

1. In a large resealable plastic bag, combine beef, 2 tbsp oil and brandy. Season with salt and pepper. Seal bag tightly and refrigerate for 3 hours.
2. Preheat oven to 300°F with a rack in the middle of the oven.
3. In a large, heavy-bottom casserole dish over medium-high heat, add oil and heat until shimmering. Add carrots, onions, mushrooms, garlic, orange zest and 1/2 tsp salt, stirring well. Reduce heat to low, cover and cook 10 minutes or until onions and garlic are softened.
4. Add beef and marinade to the dish. Stir in tomatoes, wine, parsley, thyme and peppercorns, stirring well to combine.
5. Cover casserole and bake 5 to 6 hours. Meat should be fork-tender.
6. Season to taste with salt and pepper. Serve immediately. Alternatively, refrigerate dish overnight. Skim any congealed fat from the top. Reheat and serve.

Serving Suggestion
* Serve over egg noodles.

Pork Chops with Vegetable Medley

Zucchini and tomatoes abound in this delightful dish of seared meaty pork chops. Fresh oregano and black olives give this dish a unique spin.

Makes 4 Servings

Calories 258 | Carbohydrate 102 g | Fiber 2 g | Fat 16 g | Protein 19 g

4 boneless rib pork chops, or center-cut, about 1 inch thick
Kosher salt
Freshly ground black pepper
2 tbsp olive oil
2 medium zucchini, cut into 3/4-inch pieces
3 cloves garlic, minced
3/4 cup low-sodium chicken broth
1 tbsp chopped fresh oregano
2 cups cherry tomatoes, halved
1/3 cup pitted black olives, halved

Tips
*   To prevent your chops from curling up at the edges, before browning make a few tiny cuts in the fat and skin around the edges, without cutting into the meat.

1. Season pork chops with salt and pepper. In a large skillet, add 1 tbsp oil and cook over medium-high heat until shimmering. Add pork chops and cook, turning once, 7 minutes until browned and pink in the center. Transfer chops to plate and cover with foil.

2. Add remaining oil to the skillet and heat until shimmering. Add zucchini and season with salt; cook, stirring often, about 4 minutes until browned. Add garlic and cook, stirring, 1 minute. Add broth and oregano; cook, scraping up any browned bits from the bottom of the pan, 1 minute. Move zucchini to edges of pan. Return chops and any accumulated juices to pan; cook, turning chops occasionally, 7 minutes or until pork is no longer pink in the middle and sauce is slightly thickened. Transfer chops to a serving platter.

3. Add tomatoes and olives to the skillet and cook, tossing gently, 1 minute or until warmed through. Season to taste with salt and pepper. Spoon vegetable mixture over the chops. Serve warm.

Roasted Garlic Dijon Pork Loin

This delicious entrée is made with tender roasted pork loin that is drizzled with a refreshing lemon and herb vinaigrette

Makes 6 to 8 Servings

Calories 284 | Carbohydrate 1 g | Fiber 0 g | Fat 9 g | Protein 99 g

2-1/2 tbsp virgin olive oil, divided
1 pork loin roast (about 2-1/2 to 3 lbs)
Kosher salt
Freshly ground black pepper
2 tbsp minced garlic
1 tbsp crushed oregano leaves
1 tbsp Dijon mustard

1. Preheat oven to 350°F.
2. In a large skillet over medium-high heat, add 1 tbsp oil and heat until shimmering. Season pork with salt and pepper. Add pork to the skillet and cook, turning occasionally, 8 to 10 minutes or until browned on all side.
3. Meanwhile, in a small bowl, add 2 tsp oil, garlic, oregano, mustard, 1/2 tsp salt and 1/2 tsp pepper, blending well into a paste.
4. Brush paste all over pork. Transfer pork to a foil-line baking sheet.
5. Roast pork 45 minutes or until an instant-read thermometer inserted horizontally into the roast registers 145°F for medium-rare to medium. Transfer pork to a cutting board, cover with foil and let stand 10 minutes.
6. Slice pork across the grain. Transfer to a serving platter and serve immediately.

Roasted Pork, Asparagus and Tomatoes

This completely satisfying Mediterranean dish of pork tenderloin, a balance of tasty vegetables and a lemon-thyme vinaigrette is easy to make.

Makes 4 Servings

Calories 274 | Carbohydrate 7 g | Fiber 3 g | Fat 16 g | Protein 26 g

1 lb pork tenderloin, trimmed
1 tsp dried marjoram
1/4 tsp ground pepper
2 tbsp vegetable oil, divided
1 lb fresh asparagus, trimmed and cut into 1-inch pieces
1 large red onion, chopped
1 cup halved cherry tomatoes
Vinaigrette
1 large cloves garlic, minced
1 tsp minced fresh thyme leaves
2 tbsp fresh lemon juice
1/8 tsp kosher salt
4 tsp extra virgin olive oil
Freshly ground black pepper

Serving Suggestion
* Serve with a rice pilaf or a side salad.

1. Preheat oven to 400°F.
2. Season pork with marjoram, pepper and 1/4 tsp salt. In a large oven-proof skillet over medium-high add 1 tbsp oil and heat until shimmering. Add the pork and cook, turning often, about 5 to 7 minutes or until browned all over.
3. In a medium bowl, add the asparagus, onion and remaining oil and salt, mixing well. Arrange mixture around the pork.
4. Roast pork and vegetables, adding tomatoes halfway through, 12 minutes or until an instant-read thermometer inserted horizontally in the pork registers 155°F for medium-rare to medium.
5. Transfer pork to a cutting board, cover with foil and let stand 5 minutes. Stir vegetables with the juices in the skillet.
6. *Vinaigrette:* In a small bowl, whisk together the garlic, thyme, lemon juice and salt. Slowly whisk in the olive oil.
7. Slice pork, across the grain, into 1-inch medallions. Transfer pork to serving plates. Arrange vegetables around the pork. Serve drizzled with vinaigrette. Season to taste with pepper.

PASTA

Whole Grain Lasagna with Eggplant and Olives

This Italian whole-grain pasta makes preparing a delicious and healthy family meal quick and easy.

Makes 6 Servings

Calories 324 | Carbohydrate 40 g | Fiber 9 g | Fat 14 g | Protein 12 g

6 whole-grain lasagna
  sheets
1/4 cup olive oil
2 small eggplant, peeled
  and diced
1 onion, diced
2 small carrots, diced
1 red bell pepper,
  seeded and diced
18 black olives, pitted
  and finely chopped
2 cloves garlic, minced
1 tbsp finely chopped
  fresh cilantro leaves
1/4 tsp kosher salt
1/4 cup water
1 cup shredded low-fat
  mozzarella cheese
3/4 cup tomato sauce

1. Preheat the oven to 350°F.
2. Cook the lasagna al dente according to package directions. Drain and rinse with cool water. Let cool on a work surface.
3. In a large sauté pan over medium heat, add the oil and heat until shimmering. Add the eggplant, onion, carrot, bell pepper, olives, garlic, cilantro, salt and water; cook, stirring occasionally, 8 minutes or until the vegetables are tender.
4. Spoon about 2 tbsp of the eggplant mixture and 4 tsp of the mozzarella down the middle of each noodle, stopping 1 inch before the ends. Starting with the end closest to you, roll each noodle up and then secure with a toothpick.
5. In a greased 11- by 7-inch glass baking dish, arrange the rollups. Spoon the tomato sauce over the top. Sprinkle with the remaining cheese.
6. Bake 15 to 20 minutes or until the cheese is golden brown.

Hearty Lasagna with Lentils and Zucchini

This is a quick and easy way to add an Italian influence to a healthy and enjoyable Mediterranean meal.

Makes 8 Servings

Calories 331 | Carbohydrate 48 g | Fiber 13 g | Fat 8 g | Protein 19 g

1 cup dry whole lentils, rinsed
3 cups water
1-1/4 tsp fennel seeds
2 cans (15.5 oz) low-sodium tomato sauce
1/8 tsp granulated sugar
1 tsp dried basil leaves, crushed
1 tsp kosher salt
8 oz whole grain lasagna noodles
2 tbsp virgin olive oil
2 cups chopped onion
3 large cloves garlic, minced
2 zucchini, sliced
1-1/2 cups low fat shredded mozzarella cheese

1. In a large pot, combine the lentils, water and fennel seeds. Bring to a boil, reduce the heat, cover, and simmer for 15 to 20 minutes, or until the lentils are tender. Drain. Stir in the tomato sauce, sugar, basil and salt. Set aside.
2. Cook noodles according to the package directions.
3. Preheat the oven to 350°F.
4. In a large skillet over medium heat, and 1-1/2 tbsp of oil and heat until shimmering. Add the onions and cook, stirring often, 5 to 7 minutes or until softened. Add the garlic and cook, stirring, 1 minute or until the garlic is fragrant. Transfer mixture to a bowl and set aside.
5. Add the remaining oil to the skillet and heat over medium heat until shimmering. Add the zucchini and cook, turning, 8 minutes or until the zucchini are just tender.
6. Lightly oil a 13- by 9-inch glass baking dish. Arrange half of the lasagna noodles on the bottom of the dish. Layer the zucchini, half of the lentils and 3/4 cup cheese. Layer the remaining noodles, the onion mixture and the remaining lentils.
7. Cover with foil and bake 30 minutes or until heated through. Uncover and sprinkle with the remaining cheese. Bake, uncovered, 5 minutes or until the cheese is melted and golden brown.

Baked Rigatoni and Cauliflower

This recipe is sure to add mouth-watering flavors to cauliflower with rigatoni and these carefully selected herbs and spices.

Makes 8 Servings

Calories 406 | Carbohydrate 51 g | Fiber 4 g | Fat 14 g | Protein 17 g

1 lb whole-grain rigatoni

1 medium cauliflower (about 1 1/2 lbs)

1/4 cup virgin olive oil, divided

Kosher salt

Freshly ground black pepper

1 tbsp capers, coarsely chopped

3 cloves garlic, minced

3 tbsp coarsely chopped sage

½ tsp lemon zest

¼ tsp red pepper flakes

6 ozs grated mozzarella cheese

2 oz grated Romano cheese

½ cup coarse dry bread crumbs

2 tbsp chopped flat-leaf parsley

1. Cook the rigatoni according to package directions to al dente. Drain. Rinse with cool water, drain and set aside.

2. Preheat oven to 400°F. Cut cauliflower from top to bottom and remove core. Lay cut sides down and cut cauliflower horizontally into 1/4-inch slices. Break into small chunks.

3. In a large skillet over medium-high heat, add 3 tbsp oil and heat until shimmering. Working in batches, arrange the cauliflower in 1 layer and cook, 2 minutes or until browned. Flip cauliflower over and cook, 2 minutes or until cauliflower is easily pierced with a fork. Transfer to a large mixing bowl and repeat with remaining cauliflower.

4. Return cauliflower to the skillet. Season with salt and pepper. Stir in capers, garlic, sage, lemon zest and pepper flakes.

5. Return cauliflower mixture to the large mixing bowl. Add rigatoni and mozzarella, tossing well. Transfer mixture to a lightly greased 8-cup casserole dish. Sprinkle with Romano cheese and bread crumbs. Drizzle with the remaining oil.

6. Bake 20 to 30 minutes or until top is golden and bubbly. Serve garnished with parsley.

Pasta Primavera

This Italian inspired meal uses whole grain fettuccine and an assortment of nutritious vegetables to produce a large, delicious, and healthy meal.

Makes 8 Servings

Calories 373 | Carbohydrate 54 g | Fiber 5 g | Fat 10 g | Protein 14 g

1 lb whole grain
    fettuccine
3 tbsp virgin olive oil
1-1/2 lbs asparagus,
    trimmed and cut into
    1-inch pieces
2 carrots, thinly sliced
1 cup small broccoli
    florets
1-1/2 cups frozen peas
3 onions, chopped
1 cup lightly packed
    baby spinach leaves
Sauce:
1/2 cup vegetable broth
1/4 cup dry white wine
1/2 cup crème fraîche
1/2 cup grated
    Parmigiano-Reggiano
1/2 lemon, juice of
Kosher salt
Freshly ground black
    pepper
Fresh parsley leaves

1. Cook fettucine according to the package directions. Drain pasta. Transfer to a large bowl and toss with 2 tbsp oil. Set aside.

2. In a large skillet over medium heat, add the remaining oil and heat until shimmering. Add the asparagus, carrots and broccoli; cook, stirring often, 5 minutes or until the vegetables begin to soften. Stir in the peas, onions and spinach; cook, stirring often, 3 minutes. Transfer the vegetables to a large bowl.

3. In the same skillet over medium heat, add the broth and wine; cook for 3 to 4 minutes until the liquid has reduced by half. Stir in the crème fraîche, Parmigiano-Reggiano and lemon juice. Season to taste with salt and pepper. Add the vegetable mixture to the sauce and simmer, stirring often, 3 minutes or until flavors are melded. Pour mixture over the fettuccine, tossing to coat.

4. Serve garnished with parsley.

Farfalle with Tomato Avocado Sauce

Italian whole grain farfalle served with a tasty, full-flavor tomato and avocado sauce is a quick and simple way to prepare a meal to satisfy every hungry appetite.

Makes 8 Servings

Calories 361 | Carbohydrate 49 g | Fiber 6 g | Fat 14 g | Protein 10 g

1 lb whole grain farfalle
4 cloves garlic
3 tbsp extra virgin olive oil
1 lemon, juice of
2 ripe avocados, peeled and pitted
1 roma tomato, chopped
1/2 cup chopped fresh basil
Kosher salt
Freshly ground black pepper
Parmigiano-Reggiano cheese

1. Cook farfalle according to package directions.
2. Meanwhile in a blender, combine the garlic, olive oil and lemon juice and blend until smooth. Add the avocados, tomato and basil and blend until smooth. Season with salt and pepper.
3. Drain the pasta. Transfer to serving bowls and drizzle with sauce. Serve garnished with Parmigiano-Reggiano.

Tuna with Farfalle and Artichokes

Preparing tuna steaks with farfalle, artichoke hearts, tomatoes, fresh herbs, and a touch of white wine brings out the wonderful flavors and textures of each ingredient.

Makes 4 Servings

Calories 345 | Carbohydrate 27 g | Fiber 5 g | Fat 17 g | Protein 18 g

1/4 cup virgin olive oil, divided

2 tsp freshly grated lemon zest

2 tsp chopped fresh rosemary

1 tsp Kosher salt

1/2 tsp freshly ground black pepper

6 ozs tuna steaks, about 3/4-inch thick, cut into 2 equal pieces

4 oz farfalle pasta

1/4 cup chopped green olives

3 cloves garlic, minced

2 cups grape tomatoes, halved

1/2 cup white wine

2 tbsp lemon juice

1/2 10 oz package frozen artichoke hearts, thawed and patted dry

Chopped fresh parsley

1. In a large bowl, combine 1 tbsp oil, lemon zest, 1 tsp rosemary, 1/4 tsp salt and the pepper. Set aside.

2. In a large heavy-bottom skillet over medium-high heat, add 2 tsp oil and heat until shimmering. Add the tuna and cook, turning once, 6 to 8 minutes or until tuna flakes easily when tested with a fork. Transfer tuna to lemon mixture, turning to coat. When cool enough to handle, break tuna into 1-inch chunks.

3. Meanwhile, cook farfalle according to package directions. Drain and set aside.

4. In a large skillet over medium heat, add the remaining oil and heat until shimmering. Stir in artichoke hearts, olives, garlic and the remaining rosemary; cook, stirring, 3 minutes or until the garlic is beginning to brown. Add tomatoes and wine; bring to a boil and cook, stirring occasionally, 3 minutes or until the tomatoes are softened and the mixture has reduced slightly.

5. Stir in the farfalle, tuna, lemon juice and the remaining salt. Cook, gently stirring, about 1 to 2 minutes or until heated through. Serve garnished with parsley.

Tuna, Green Beans & Tomatoes with Shells

This Italian-inspired meal can be easily prepared and served within a few short minutes.

Makes 4 Servings

Calories 386 | Carbohydrate 50 g | Fiber 5 g | Fat 11 g | Protein 23 g

8 oz whole grain medium pasta shells
8 oz green beans, trimmed cut in half
2 tbsp virgin olive oil
2 cloves garlic, sliced
8 oz cherry tomatoes, halved
2 cans (5 oz) tuna packed in water, drained
1/2 cup kalamata olives, coarsely chopped
1/2 cup lightly packed chopped fresh basil
Kosher salt
Freshly ground black pepper
Fat free Parmigiano-Reggiano cheese

1. Cook pasta according to package directions. 2 minutes before the pasta is done, add the beans and cook until pasta is al dente. Reserve 1/2 cup pasta water and set aside. Drain the shells and beans.

2. In a large skillet over medium heat, add the oil and heat until shimmering. Add the garlic and cook, stirring, 1 minute or until fragrant. Add the tomatoes, tuna, olives, basil and pasta water, stirring and flaking tuna with a fork, until combined. Add pasta and beans, stirring well. Season to taste with salt and pepper.

3. Transfer pasta mixture to serving bowls. Serve garnished with parmesan.

Tuscan Baked Ziti

Makes 6 Servings

Calories 489 | Carbohydrate 76 g | Fiber 7 g | Fat 10 g | Protein 21 g

3 cups whole grain ziti
8 oz shredded Italian cheese blend, divided
2 red bell peppers, cored, seeded and cut into 1/4-inch strips
2 zucchini, halved lengthwise and sliced crosswise
8 oz sliced button mushrooms
1 jar (24 oz) pasta sauce
1 tbsp chopped fresh oregano

1 Preheat oven to 375°F.

2. Cook pasta according to package directions. Drain and transfer to a large bowl. Stir in 1-1/4 cups cheese, bell peppers, zucchini, mushrooms, pasta sauce and oregano.

3. Spray a 13 - by 9-inch baking dish with nonstick cooking spray. Spoon pasta mixture into dish. Sprinkle with remaining cheese.

4. Bake 20 to 25 minutes or until heated through and cheese is melted. Remove from oven.

5. Let stand 5 minutes before serving.

DESSERTS

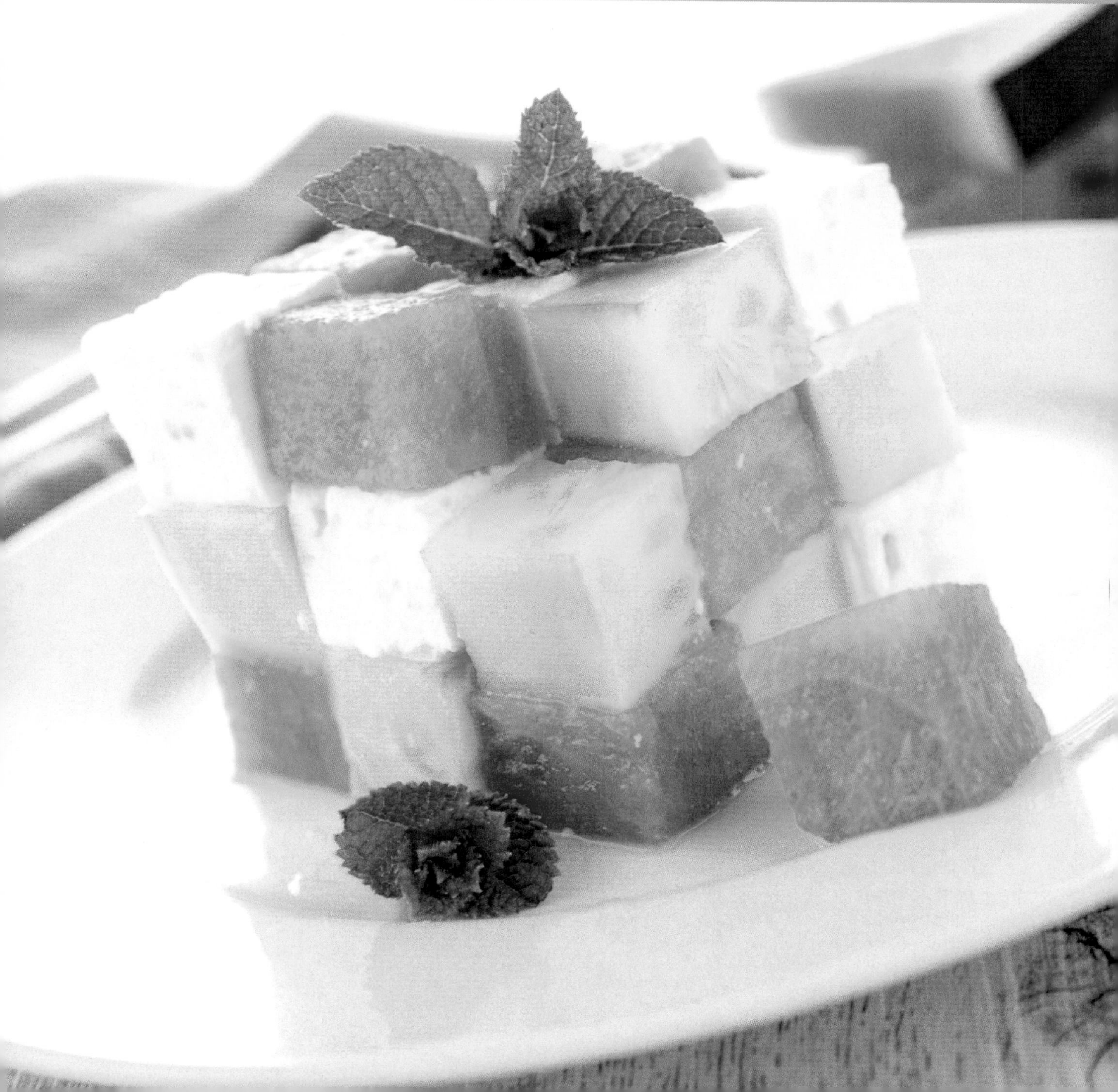

Yogurt Panna Cotta with Honey

Panna cotta is a delightful molded chilled dessert that is popular throughout the Mediterranean. This version uses yogurt and low fat milk in place of the heavy creams.

Makes 6 Servings

Calories 232 | Carbohydrate 48 g | Fiber 0 g | Fat 2 g | Protein 8 g

1-1/2 tsp unflavored gelatin
1 tbsp water
1 cup fat-free milk
1/3 cup granulated sugar
1 cup low-fat buttermilk
1 cup fat-free plain Greek yogurt
2 tbsp honey
Raspberries, blackberries or grapes

1. In a small bowl, mix the gelatin with the water and let stand 5 minutes or until softened.
2. In a small saucepan over medium heat, add the milk and heat until simmering. Add the sugar and cook, stirring, 1 minute or until the sugar is dissolved. Remove from the heat. Stir in the softened gelatin until dissolved.
3. In a medium bowl, whisk the buttermilk and the yogurt. Whisk in the milk mixture until smooth. Pour into six 4-oz ramekins. Refrigerate 3 hours or until set.
4. Drizzle panna cottas with honey. Serve garnished with raspberries, blackberries or grapes.

Berries and Honey Ginger Yogurt

Greek yogurt blended with a delicate mix of orange zest, crushed ginger and honey served over fresh berries is a quick and easy-to-prepare desert that is sure to be a favorite.

Makes 4 Servings

Calories 375 | Carbohydrate 59 g | Fiber 9 g | Fat 12 g | Protein 11 g

16 oz plain Greek yogurt
1/3 cup honey
1 orange, zest of
5 pieces crystallized ginger, crushed
8 oz blackberries
8 oz raspberries
8 oz strawberries, hulled and sliced

1. In a medium bowl, combine the yogurt, 3 tbsp honey, orange zest and ginger. Let stand 5 minutes.
2. Evenly divide the blackberries, raspberries and strawberries into 4 dessert bowls. Top each with a large dollop of the yogurt mixture.
3. Serve drizzled, to taste, with the remaining honey.

Jeweled Fruit en Papillote

This delicious desert that features fruit wrapped in parchment and roasted will prove to be refreshing and extremely satisfying. When garnished with Greek yogurt and served with a sprinkling of maple sugar the end result is divine.

Makes 4 Servings

Calories 215 | Carbohydrate 42 g | Fiber 6 g | Fat 4 g | Protein 5 g

4 apricots, halved and sliced into quarters

1 honeydew melon, chopped into large pieces

1 peach, halved and sliced into quarters

4 cinnamon sticks

4 whole vanilla beans

4 tsp dry red wine

1/2 cup plain Greek yogurt

2 tsp maple sugar

1. Preheat oven to 400°F.
2. Cut 4 large sheets of parchment paper. Divide apricots, melon and peaches and pomegranate seeds evenly into the center of each piece of parchment paper.
3. Top each mound of fruit with a cinnamon stick, vanilla bean and 1 tsp wine.
4. Bring up opposite edges of the parchment paper and fold edges a few times to seal tightly. Fold up the remaining ends of the parchment, sealing tightly.
5. Transfer parchment packs to a baking sheet. Bake 20 minutes or until the fruit is tender.
6. Cut open the parchment packets and transfer the fruit and any accumulated juices to serving plates. Serve garnished with yogurt and sprinkled with maple sugar.

Note: Fruit can be served in packets, if desired. Cut packet open before serving.

Fruit Cup Chia Pudding

This is an easy-to-make refreshing desert made with healthy cantaloupe, bananas, protein laden chia seeds, and cashews is certain to become a favorite.

Makes 6 Servings

Calories 324 | Carbohydrate 38 g | Fiber 10 g | Fat 18 g | Protein 7 g

1 cantaloupe, seeded and cut into 6 wedges
5 cups water (approx.)
2/3 cup chia seeds
4 bananas
1⁄2 cup whole cashews
1/2 cup coconut cream
1/4 tsp pure vanilla extract
Mint leaves

1. Cut checkerboard-style slices into the bottom of each cantaloupe section, without cutting through the rind. Set aside.
2. In a large bowl, combine 4 cups water and chia seeds. Let stand, stirring occasionally, 25 minutes or until thickened and smooth.
3. Using a blender, combine bananas, cashews, coconut cream and vanilla extract. Blend in water until mixture reaches 4 cups and is the consistency of custard cream.
4. Transfer cantaloupe quarters onto servings plates. Spoon chia pudding, evenly divided, over the top of each. Pour the banana cream mixture over the top.
5. Serve garnished with mint leaves.

Apple Granola and Yogurt Mini Trifle

Diced apples toasted with tasty granola and served with Greek yogurt topped with raisins and crushed walnuts quickly becomes a delicious and healthy Mediterranean-inspired desert.

Makes 6 Servings

Calories 312 | Carbohydrate 30 g | Fiber 5 g | Fat 17 g | Protein 11 g

2 tbsp chopped walnuts
2 cups granola or muesli
1-1/3 cups Greek yogurt
1 cup diced tart apples
1-1/2 tbsp raisins

Tip
* In place of trifle dishes, use wide drinking glasses or wide-mouth canning jars.

1. In a skillet over medium-high heat, add the walnuts and toast, swirling, 2 minutes or until fragrant. Set aside to cool.
2. In each trifle dish, layer 1/2 cup granola, 6 tbsp yogurt, 1/4 cup apples and repeat. Top each with half of the walnuts and raisins.

Dates with Yogurt, Citrus and Honey

This naturally sweet desert combines healthy dates, oranges, honey, pistachios, and Greek yogurt into an inviting and satisfying delicacy

Makes 2 Servings

Calories 344 | Carbohydrate 66 g | Fiber 10 g | Fat 4 g | Protein 16 g

1 cup plain nonfat Greek yogurt

2 medium oranges, peeled

2 tbsp honey

2 dates, preferably Medjool, pitted and chopped

2 tbsp chopped pistachios

1. Divide yogurt between 2 bowls.
2. Cut ends off of oranges.Slice orange into circles and then cut circles in half. Arrange over yogurt.
3. Drizzle each serving with honey.
4. Serve sprinkled with dates and pistachios.

Dried Figs with Ricotta and Walnuts

Dried figs with ricotta cheese, honey, and walnuts quickly become a refreshing Mediterranean-style desert or a healthy, on-the-run snack.

Makes 4 Servings

Calories 101 | Carbohydrate 16 g | Fiber 2 g | Fat 3 g | Protein 3 g

16 walnut halves

8 dried figs

1/4 cup part skim ricotta cheese

1 tbsp honey

1. In a skillet over medium-high heat, add the walnuts and toast, swirling, 2 minutes or until fragrant. Set aside to cool.
2. Cut figs in half crosswise and arrange on serving plate, cut side up.
3. Using a spoon, make a small indentation on the cut side of each fig. Spoon about 3/4 tsp ricotta cheese onto the top of each fig. Arrange walnut halves on top of each.
4. Serve drizzled with honey

Cherry Clafoutis

This delicious desert, introduced to us by the inimitable Juilia Child is a unique light crepe-like batter that is embedded with sweet cherries for an elegant dessert that is surprisingly simplet to make.

Makes 8 Servings

Calories 215 | Carbohydrate 38 g | Fiber 2 g | Fat 5 g | Protein 4 g

Butter

1-1⁄4 pounds sweet cherries, stemmed and pitted

3 large eggs, room temperature

1⁄2 cup all-purpose flour

1 tsp pure vanilla extract

1 tsp grated lemon zest

3/4 cup granulated sugar (approx.)

1⁄3 cup milk

1. Preheat oven to 375°F.
2. Liberally butter an 8-cup shallow baking dish. Arrange cherries in a single layer.
3. Using a blender, mix the eggs, flour, vanilla extract, lemon zest, 1/2 cup sugar and milk until smooth. Pour the batter over the cherries. Sprinkle with 3 tbsp sugar.
4. Bake clafoutis 45 minutes or until the custard is set and a knife inserted in the center comes out mostly clean.
5. Serve warm, at room temperature or chilled.

Tip
* The clafoutis can be made up to 24 hours ahead of time; covered and refrigerated.

Variation
* Substitute equal amounts of raspberries or blackberries for the cherries.

Turkish Yogurt Cake

This delicious desert is very rich like cheesecake but contains dried fruit and Greek yogurt for a healthier dessert with a Mediterranean flair.

Makes 6 Servings

Calories 340 | Carbohydrate 40 g | Fiber 2 g | Fat 15 g | Protein 14 g

1/4 cup golden raisins, roughly chopped
Muscat or sherry
5 large eggs, separated
1/3 cup granulated sugar
3 tbsp honey
3/4 cups white whole flour
2 cups plain Greek yogurt
1 lemon, zest and juice of
1 tbsp virgin olive oil

1. Preheat oven to 350°F.
2. Grease an 8-inch springform pan.
3. In a small bowl, add the raisins and cover with room temperature water. Let stand 10 minutes. Drain and set aside.
3. Using a mixer, in a medium bowl, beat the egg yolks, sugar and honey until thick and creamy. Carefully add the flour, raisins, yogurt, lemon zest, lemon juice and oil, mixing on low until well combined.
4. In a separate bowl, mix the egg whites until stiff. Stir in a large spoonful of the egg white mixture into the egg yolk mixture. Gently fold in the remaining egg whites.
5. Pour mixture into the prepared pan. Bake 50 to 60 minutes or until the top is browned and the cake is puffed up in the center. Transfer to a wire rack and let cool.
6. When the cake starts to pull away from the sides of the pan, loosen the remaining cake with a knife and open the springform. Let stand until completedly cool.
7. Cut into six wedges and serve.

Strawberry Granita

This refreshing granita is so amazingly easy to make, it may become your new go-to dessert or snack. It is low in calories, yet entirely satisfying.

Makes 6 Servings (about 4 cups)

Calories 126 | Carbohydrate 32 g | Fiber 2 g | Fat 0 g | Protein 1 g

1 cupwater
3/4 cup granulated sugar
2 tbsplemon juice
3 cupshulled and sliced strawberries (about 1 lb) plus more berries for garnish, if desired
Fresh mint leaves (optional)

Tip
* After step 5, the Granita can be covered tightly and frozen for up to 2 days.

1. In a medium saucepan over medium heat add the water and sugar; cook, stirring often, until sugar is dissolved.
2. Add strawberries to a blender or food processor and process until smooth. Add syrup, blending until combined.
3. Pour the mixture into a 13-by 9-by 2-inch metal baking pan. Freeze about 30 minutes or until icy around the edges.
4. Using a fork, stir icy parts into the center of the mixture. Return to freezer, stirring edges into the center every 25 to 30 minutes, about 2 to 3 hours or until mixture is completely frozen.
5. Scrape granita into icy flakes. Cover tightly and freeze until ready to use.
6. To serve, scrape granita into bowls and garnish with additional berries or mint leaves, if desired.

Variation:

Lemon Granita: Increase water to 1-1/2 cups, sugar to 1 cup and lemon juice to 1 cup. Omit the strawberries. Add 2 sprigs fresh thymes leaves. Add all ingredients in step 1. Omit step 2. Remove thyme sprigs before transferring freezing. Continue with remaining steps. Garnish with lemon rind curls, if desired.

Strawberry Topped Almond Cake

This gluten-free cake made with almond flower is fluffy and moist while boasting high nutrient values. Top it with slices berries for a delicious desert or an inviting snack.

Makes 12 Servings

Calories 165 | Carbohydrate 16 g | Fiber 2 g | Fat 9 g | Protein 6 g

2/3 cup sugar divided
4 large eggs separated
1 teaspoon vanilla extract
1 1/2 cups almond flour
1 teaspoon baking powder
1/4 teaspoon salt
1 1/2-2 cups sliced strawberries
Greek yogurt (optional)

1. Preheat oven to 350°F. Lightly grease an 8-inch round pan with butter. Sprinkle 1-1/2 tbsp sugar into the bottom of the pan.
2. In a large mixing bowl, whisk together the egg yolks, 1/4 cup of the sugar and the vanilla until smooth.
3. Using a stand mixer, whip the egg whites until they form soft peaks. Slowly beat in the remaining 1/4 cup sugar. Set aside.
4. Whisk together the almond flour, coconut flour, baking powder and salt. Combine with the egg yolk mixture, stirring until a thick dough forms. Working in 3 batches, fold in the egg whites, combining fully between each batch.
5. Pour the batter into the prepared pan. Bake for 30 to 35 minutes or until golden brown and a tester inserted into the center comes out clean.
6. Let cake stand 10 minutes or slightly cool. Run a knife around the edge of the cake. Let stand until cool.
7. Serve topped with strawberries and a dollop of yogurt (if using).

MEASUREMENT EQUIVALENTS

1 tablespoon (tbsp) =	3 teaspoons (tsp)	1 cup =	48 tsp
1/16 cup =	1 tbsp	1 cup =	16 tbsp
1/8 cup =	2 tbsp	8 fluid ounces (oz) =	1 cup
1/4 cup =	4 tbsp	2 cups =	1 pint (pt)
1/3 cup =	5 tbsp + 1 tsp	2 pints =	1 quart (qt)
3/4 cup =	6 tbsp	1 quart =	4 cups
1/2 cup =	8 tbsp	4 quarts =	1 gallon
2/3 cup =	10 tbsp + 2 tsp	(gal)	
3/4 cup =	12 tbsp		

Imperial (US) to Metric (Modern UK) Volume

1/8 tsp	0.5 mL	2/3 cup	150 mL
1/4 tsp	1 mL	3/4 cup	175 mL
1/2 tsp	2 mL	1 cup	250 mL
3/4 tsp	3 mL	1-1/4 cups	300 mL
1 tsp	5 mL	1-1/3 cups	325 mL
1-1/4 tsp	6 mL	1-1/2 cups	375 mL
1-1/2 tsp	7 mL	1-2/3 cups	400 mL
1-3/4 tsp	8 mL	1-3/4 cups	425 mL
2 tsp	10 mL	2 cups	500 mL
2-1/2 tsp	12 mL	2-1/2 cups	625 mL
1 tbsp	15 mL	3 cups	750 mL
1-1/2 tbsp	22 mL	3-1/2 cups	875 mL
2 tbsp	30 mL	4 cups	1 L
3 tbsp	45 mL	5 cups	1.25 L
1/4 cup	60 mL	6 cups	1.5 L
1/3 cup	75 mL	7 cups	1.75 L
6 tbsp	90 mL	8 cups	2 L
1/2 cup	125 mL		

Weight

1/4 oz	7 g	8 oz	250 g
1/2 oz	15 g	10 oz	300 g
1 oz	30 g	12 oz	375 g
1-1/2 oz	45 g	1 lb	500 g
2 oz	60 g	1-1/4 lbs	625 g
2-1/2 oz	75 g	1-1/2 lbs	750 g
3 oz	90 g	2 lbs	1 kg
4 oz	125 g	3 lbs	1.5 kg
5 oz	150 g	3-1/2 lbs	1.75 kg
6 oz	175 g	4 lbs	2 kg
7 oz	210 g		

Length

1/16 inch	2 mm	3 inches	7.5 cm
1/8 inch	3 mm	4 inches	10 cm
1/4 inch	0.5 cm	5 inches	12.5 cm
1/2 inch	1 cm	6 inches	15 cm
3/4 inch	2 cm	7 inches	18 cm
1 inch	2.5 cm	8 inches	20 cm
1-1/2 inches	4 cm	9 inches	23 cm
2 inches	5 cm	10 inches	25 cm
2-1/2 inches	6 cm	12 inches	30 cm

Oven Temperatures

140°F	60°C	350°F	180°C
150°F	70°C	375°F	190°C
170°F	80°C	400°F	200°C
200°F	100°C	425°F	220°C
250°F	120°C	450°F	230°C
275°F	140°C	475°F	240°C
300°F	150°C	500°F	260°C
325°F	160°C		

ABOUT THE AUTHOR

Marilyn Haugen is an author, recipe developer, business owner and former finance director at American Express. She has authored several bestselling cookbooks, including 150 Best Spiralizer Recipes, 5-Ingredient Instant Pot Cookbook and 175 Best Instant Pot Recipes. She is the founder of FoodThymes.com, a food blog dedicated to sharing delicious, quick and healthy meals without all the hassles.

Working in Corporate America, required her to travel frequently around the world. While dining in restaurants for almost every meal, not only did she experience amazing cuisine and cultures, but she developed a love and appreciation for home cooked meals.

Above all, she loved to cook, entertain and explore new cuisines and cooking techniques. Some of her best experiences have been cooking and sharing meals together with family and friends. So why shouldn't that be the next logical step as a career path when starting her entrepreneurial journey? She wondered if it could be true that she could justify her obsession with small appliances, gadgets and trying out new recipes. Would all the endless hours of researching cooking methods, reading food magazines and collecting cookbooks have a purpose other than sheer entertainment? She decided to find out.

Since that time, she has written over 12 cookbooks, several of which have been published by large corporate publishers and others which she has self-published. All her books are well researched and the recipes tested and refined.

In The Mediterranean Diet Cookbook for Healthy Living she hopes you will be able to take away some great recipes that you, your family or friends will truly appreciate.

If you enjoyed this book, I would really appreciate your honest review. Your reviews are extremely helpful to authors and I do read all of them. If you have any questions or comments, drop me a note at FoodThymes.com

Marilyn

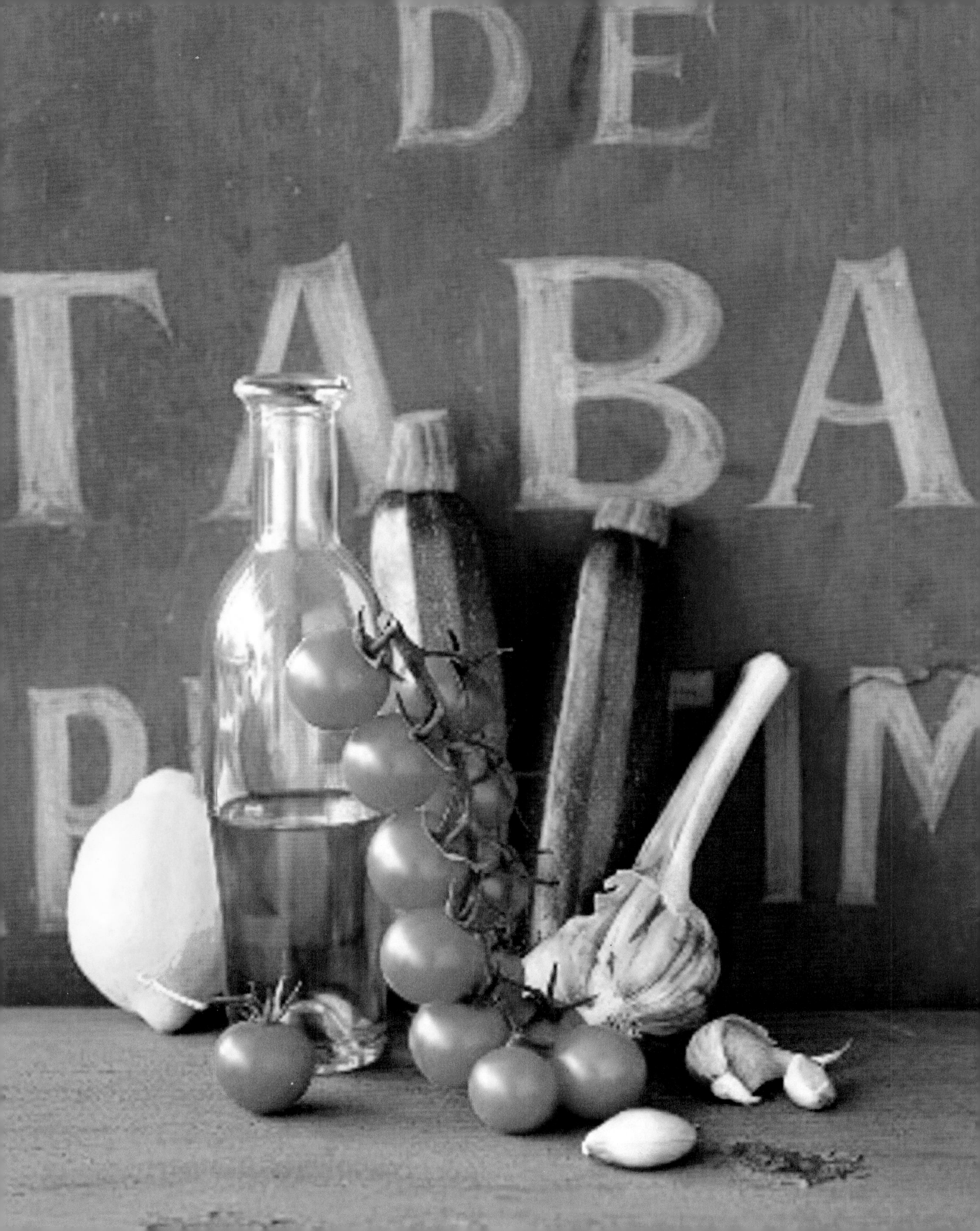
DE
TABA

Made in the USA
Middletown, DE
02 April 2019